THE ULTIMATE

SPAM®
BRAND

COOKBOOK

EXPANDED EDITION

140+ Quick and Delicious Recipes from Traditional to Gourmet

FOX CHAPEL
PUBLISHING

SPAM trademarks are properties of Hormel Foods, LLC, used under license by Fox Chapel Publishing Company, Inc.

The Ultimate SPAM® Cookbook, Expanded Edition is a revised and expanded second edition of *The Ultimate SPAM® Cookbook* by Fox Chapel Publishing Company, Inc.

ISBN 978-1-4971-0534-8 (paperback)
ISBN 978-1-4971-0538-6 (hardcover)

Library of Congress Control Number: 2024950593

All photos and illustrations were provided by HORMEL Foods, LLC. except where noted below.

Shutterstock photos: Jacob Boomsma, 9; Sutchi, 10 (top left); Billion Photos, 10 (top center); Cozine, 10 (top right, below SPAM® Classic image); Ambient Ideas, 10 (bottom center); Andrey kariphoto, 10 (bottom right); Eremin, 10 (bottom left); Sheila Fitzgerald, 11; Andrey_Kuzmin, 198 (utensils).

Celebrity chef recipe photos and headshots, pages 154–204, are courtesy of their associated chef and used with permission.

To learn more about the other great books from Fox Chapel Publishing, or to find a retailer near you, call toll-free 800-457-9112 or visit us at *www.FoxChapelPublishing.com*. You can also send mail to:
Fox Chapel Publishing
903 Square Street
Mount Joy, PA 17552

We are always looking for talented authors. To submit an idea, please send a brief inquiry to acquisitions@foxchapelpublishing.com.

Printed in China
First printing

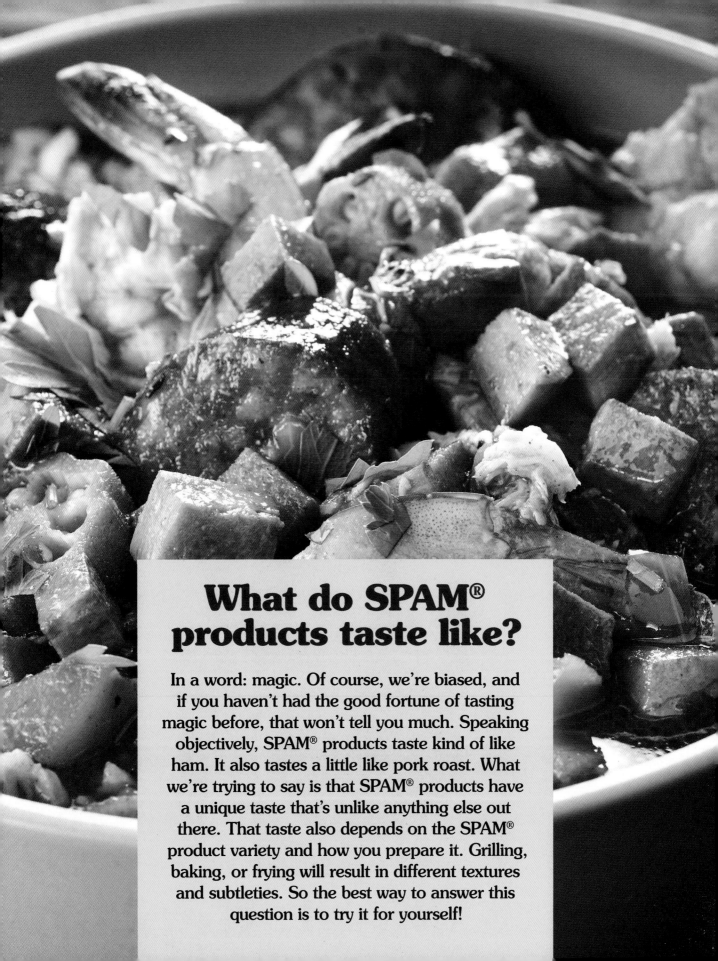

What do SPAM® products taste like?

In a word: magic. Of course, we're biased, and if you haven't had the good fortune of tasting magic before, that won't tell you much. Speaking objectively, SPAM® products taste kind of like ham. It also tastes a little like pork roast. What we're trying to say is that SPAM® products have a unique taste that's unlike anything else out there. That taste also depends on the SPAM® product variety and how you prepare it. Grilling, baking, or frying will result in different textures and subtleties. So the best way to answer this question is to try it for yourself!

Cheese. Meat. Repeat.

Contents

Foreword.. 6

What is the SPAM® Brand?.. 8

Breakfast 14

Appetizers 42

Lunch 74

Dinner...108

Desserts 148

From Chefs' Kitchens to Yours 154

Why Chefs Love SPAM® Products 198

Index...205

Foreword

I fell in love with the SPAM® brand before I ever even sampled it, and my love affair with the gelatinous cuboid of canned meat has been long-lasting. My Italian-Irish upbringing (with emphasis on the Italian when it came to food) meant it wasn't on my table when I was growing up on Long Island in the 1980s, yet I knew it was out there. I always had a fascination with products and dishes I associated so closely with Americana—things like tuna noodle casserole and mac and cheese in a box—and I thought the SPAM® brand was the leader of that gang. That colorful can, those bright, strong letters, it's pop-culture lore—it all seemed so exotic and exciting. And once I finally sought out the classic pork product and tried it, my excitement only grew.

There is just something about this canned meat. It's one of those foods that everyone has an opinion about, and those views differ depending on age, socioeconomic status, and even geographic location. Though launched at the end of the Great Depression, for many Americans it was a wartime innovation: inexpensive, shelf-stable, and convenient, perfect for the dinner table yet also ingenious for shipping overseas to become a soldier's staple. Over the years, those who relied on it during the war began to prosper, and fatigue set in on the canned pork, slowly pushing it off their plates. It began to be perceived as a lowbrow item, a pop-culture punch line—the Monty Python joke that evolved into a term for an overabundance of email. On the other hand, many Americans celebrated the staple, giving birth to festivals such as Hawaii's SPAM JAM® Festival and homages like the Austin, Minnesota SPAM® Museum. It became a beloved part of Americana, but like its birthplace the Midwest, it was looked down upon by foodies, the old-school gourmets who only saw it through a lens of kitsch.

But something happened over the years outside of mainland America. The canned meat that fed our soldiers stuck around after WWII. Postwar rations, shortages, and sanctions made proteins scarce in places like Hawaii and Japan; the Korean War extended the hardship through Southeast Asia. As those cultures began to rely on it, they incorporated SPAM® products into their own dishes, where it became a staple over the years. Most Americans probably weren't aware that overseas SPAM® products have been turned into sushi and used in fried rice, ramen, and other traditional Asian dishes. Today, SPAM® products are sold in over forty countries, with Korea being the second-largest consumer of SPAM® products in the world, after the United States. Within the United States, Hawaii consumes more SPAM® products than any other state.

Asian cuisines have recently become super-hot in the United States, and Americans are seeing a new perspective on SPAM® products. It's popping up in trendy restaurants where there seems to be a cognitive dissonance within highbrow foodies—they don't really know what to do with this thing they were so used to looking down on now that it's being used unironically by the hippest of chefs. I must admit, it's kind of fun for an old-school SPAM® brand scholar to watch this shift in perspective. It's time for a SPAM® brand renaissance!

When I was in college in the mid-1990s, I remember serving SPAM® brand and spray cheese hors-d'oeuvres to friends in my dorm room, joking that one day I'd want to throw a fancy party with fancy people where'd I'd serve SPAM® products instead of pâté. "I bet you most people wouldn't know the difference," I said. Though my own culinary tastes have evolved as I've had the opportunity to taste the world, I've always stood by the SPAM® brand. In fact, I even made the 2016 Great American SPAM® Championship award-winning SPAM® brand ice cream, brought it to a dinner party, and served it to a chef. (He liked it and ate his entire serving!)

TASTE YOU CAN HEAR.

I think my favorite part of the evolution of this popular canned pork is that all these years after my dorm-room SPAM® brand snacks, chefs in America are actually serving the canned meat with foie gras to paying customers who ordered it. And here I am writing the foreword to a book that's continuing to transform the public's perspective. So I now declare this mighty meat simultaneously highbrow and lowbrow—which means it's very special no matter how you slice it.

—Tara Cox

Executive Managing Editor, *Rachael Ray In Season* magazine

What is the SPAM® Brand?

The ads have changed over the years, but that SPAM® brand deliciousness has stayed the same!

The SPAMBURGER™ Hamburger was introduced via advertising campaigns in 1992.

History of an Icon

The first can of SPAM® brand luncheon meat came off Hormel Foods' Minnesota production line in 1937. Ken Daignaeu, brother of a Hormel Foods vice president, won a contest—and $100—for naming the SPAM® brand. But what exactly does the word "SPAM" mean? The significance of the SPAM® brand name has long been a subject of speculation. One popular belief says that it's derived from the words *spiced ham*. The real answer is known by only a small circle of former Hormel Foods executives.

The SPAM® brand was originally marketed as "The Meat of Many Uses!" and American households quickly ate it up. By 1940, 70 percent of urban Americans were eating SPAM® products. But it was the arrival of World War II, and the need for easily transported protein, that fueled the SPAM® brand's incredible growth around the world. More than 100 million pounds of SPAM® brand luncheon meat were shipped to feed Allied troops during WWII. In 1947, "The Hormel Girls," a 60-member performance troupe, toured cities across America to promote SPAM® Classic and other HORMEL® products. Americans were hooked on SPAM® products—by 1959, the one-billionth can of SPAM® Classic was produced.

The SPAM® brand has reached icon status. In America, people come from far and wide to visit the SPAM® Museum. Located in Austin, Minnesota (the birthplace of the SPAM® brand), this museum contains all things SPAM® brand, and pays tribute to its presence across the world. In 1998, SPAM® product packaging was donated to the Smithsonian. How many meat products can boast such a distinction? All of this passion and demand has amounted to this: in 2012, the eight-billionth can of SPAM® product was produced. Today, more than 9 billion cans of SPAM® products have been purchased.

The first SPAM® Museum opened in 1991 at Oak Park Mall in Austin, Minnesota, to celebrate the 100th anniversary of Hormel Foods. The current museum, pictured here, opened in 2016 in downtown Austin. There's no admission fee, and it's filled with historic SPAM® artifacts, kitschy-cool facts, and fun hands-on activities for the kids. And the gift shop is a revelation of any- and everything with that hip SPAM® brand look.

What's in a SPAM® Can?

Ah, the age-old question: what is the meat in that special can of SPAM® Classic? Many myths abound, but the answer is actually quite simple. Here's a rundown of the ingredients that make the magic.

Pork with ham: Two cuts of the pig. One perfectly tender and juicy flavor.

Salt: It's of the earth and flavors most of what we eat.

Water: Necessary to life and to SPAM® products.

Potato starch: This helps keep moisture inside the meat, where it belongs.

Sugar: It's the real deal, not that fake syrup found in other foods.

Sodium nitrite: Used to uphold the meat's high standard of quality.

How Are SPAM® Products Made?

At first glance, one might assume SPAM® products are produced through magic. But it's actually a relatively simple, conventional process.

First, the pork and ham are pre-ground. Then, salt, sugar, and the rest of the ingredients are added and mixed to reach the desired temperature. From there, the mixture is moved over to the canning line, where it's filled into the familiar metal cans, 12 ounces at a time. Once filled, cans are conveyed to a closing machine where lids are applied through vacuum sealing. Next, the cans are cooked and cooled for about three hours. At this point, they're nearly ready for enjoyment. But the cans can't leave naked. Labels are applied, and then they're off to be cased, where they await distribution.

Ready to purchase and enjoy!

HAVE A BETTER PORK-LIFE BALANCE.

How Long Can SPAM® Products Be Stored?

While the keeper of an emergency underground bunker might have you believe SPAM® products offer an eternal shelf life, there is, in fact, a limit to their goodness. On the bottom of every can of SPAM® product, you'll find a "best by" date. This is the date Hormel Foods recommends using the product by. You'll likely find yourself gobbling up the delicious meat inside the can long before that date. But if you find yourself sitting on a stock of SPAM® products during a zombie invasion, be sure to check the date before you enjoy.

Always check the date before enjoying!

DON'T KNOCK IT 'TIL YOU'VE FRIED IT.

Where Are SPAM® Products Most Popular?

In a word: everywhere!

In Southeast Asia, a SPAM® brand gift pack would be considered an appropriate wedding gift. SPAM® products are regarded as luxury goods, with gift packs selling for as much as $45 US. So if you travel there for business, leave the cigars at home and pick up this delicacy for an introductory exchange.

In Hawaii, SPAM® products are practically the national food. It's served everywhere from grocery store delis to fancy restaurants. Even McDonald's features several SPAM® items on their breakfast menu. This fanaticism fuels sales of seven million cans of SPAM® products per year in the Aloha State. The true root of the island's love for SPAM® products goes back to World War II, when the luncheon meat was served to GIs. By the end of the war, SPAM® products were adopted into local culture, with Fried SPAM® Classic and rice becoming a popular meal. The unique flavor quickly found its way into other Hawaiian cuisine, and SPAM® products became a fixture for breakfast, lunch, and dinner.

Guam may be a tiny island, but its appetite for SPAM® products is humongous. How humongous? The average annual SPAM® product consumption comes out to 16 cans per person. Guam has also been the site of SPAM® Games, where locals sample and honor the best original SPAM® recipes.

Even those blokes in the UK love SPAM® products. Of course, it's prepared in proper British style in a dish called SPAM® fritters. Similar to English fish 'n' chips, SPAM® products are dipped in batter and deep fried. Once it's good and crispy, it's ready to serve—with a sidecar of vinegar, of course.

BREAKFAST

16 SPAM® Classic and Scrambled Eggs

17 Hearty SPAM® Breakfast Skillet

18 SPAM® Loco Moco

19 SPAM® Breakfast Hash

20 SPAM® Breakfast Musubi

21 SPAM® Benedict

22 SPAM® Monkey Bread

23 Enchilada Breakfast
SPAM® Casserole

24 SPAM® Huevos Chilaquiles

25 Huevos SPAM® Cheros

26 SPAM® Breakfast Burrito

27 SPAM® Bagel Sandwich

28 SPAM® Baked French Toast

29 Ultimate SPAM® Breakfast SLT

30 SPAM® Waffle with Cheese

31 SPAM® Classic and Spinach Mini Quiches

32 SPAM® Maple Flavored Waffle
Breakfast Sandwich

33 SPAM® Maple Flavored Breakfast Bowl

34 SPAM® Western Omelet

35 Top-of-the-Morning SPAM® Breakfast Bake

36 SPAM® Maple Flavored Breakfast Poutine

37 SPAMKINS™ Breakfast Muffins

38 Spiced Dutch Baby Pancake with
SPAM® Figgy Pudding and Cranberry Butter

39 SPAM® Sriracha Benedict

40 SPAM® Frittata

41 SPAM® Classic and Waffle Musubi
with Spicy Maple Syrup

Enchilada Breakfast SPAM® Casserole

SPAM® Classic and Scrambled Eggs

 TIME: 20 MINUTES   **YIELD:** 4 SERVINGS

 Are your scrambled eggs not everything they're cracked up to be? Scramble things up with SPAM® Classic and give your taste buds a reason to get out of bed in the morning.

INGREDIENTS

- 1 (12-ounce) can SPAM® Classic, cut into cubes
- 4 large eggs
- ¼ cup milk

DIRECTIONS

1. In large non-stick skillet over medium-high heat cook SPAM® Classic slices 3 to 5 minutes or until browned and crisped. Remove from skillet.
2. In medium bowl, whisk together eggs and milk. Add to skillet. Cook egg mixture over medium-high heat, pulling with a spatula to allow the liquid to contact the skillet surface, until desired doneness.
3. Serve SPAM® Classic slices with scrambled eggs.

Hearty SPAM® Breakfast Skillet

 TIME: 30 MINUTES   **YIELD:** 6 SERVINGS

 If you want big flavor that doesn't take a big amount of time, this recipe is, well, big. A hearty helping of SPAM® Classic, potatoes, and Cheddar cheese that'll help you start the day in a big way.

INGREDIENTS

- 2 cups frozen diced or shredded potatoes
- ½ cup chopped onion
- ½ cup chopped bell pepper
- 2 teaspoons vegetable oil
- 1 (12-ounce) can SPAM® Classic, diced
- 1 (8-ounce) package frozen fat-free egg product, thawed
- ¼ teaspoon dried basil
- ⅛ teaspoon salt
- ⅛ teaspoon pepper
- 6 drops hot sauce
- ¼ cup shredded cheese

DIRECTIONS

1. In large nonstick skillet, cook potatoes, onion, and bell pepper in oil over medium-high heat, stirring constantly, 5 minutes. Add SPAM® Classic; cook and stir 5 minutes longer.

2. In small bowl, combine egg product, basil, salt, black pepper, and hot sauce; blend well. Pour over mixture in skillet; cover. Cook over medium-low heat 8 to 12 minutes or until set. Sprinkle with cheese.

SPAM® Loco Moco

 TIME: 35 MINUTES   **YIELD:** 4 SERVINGS

If you can't get two tickets to paradise, bring paradise to you! Try our SPAM® Loco Moco, a traditional breakfast from the Hawaiian Islands. With SPAM® Classic, rice, and egg, you'll wake up saying "aloha" to your mornings.

INGREDIENTS

- 1 (12-ounce) can SPAM® Classic cut into 8 slices
- 2 tablespoons butter
- 1 cup chopped cremini mushrooms
- 1 cup chopped sweet onion
- 2 cups beef broth
- 2 teaspoons Worcestershire sauce
- 2 tablespoons cornstarch
- 3 tablespoons water
- 4 cups cooked rice
- 4 eggs, cooked sunny-side up
- 3 tablespoons chopped Italian parsley
- 3 tablespoons chopped green onion
- ¼ cup diced Roma tomato, if desired

DIRECTIONS

1. In a large skillet over medium heat, cook SPAM® Classic over medium heat 3 to 5 minutes or until lightly browned and crisp. Remove from skillet.

2. In the same skillet, melt butter. Add mushrooms and onions and cook over medium-high heat for 6 to 8 minutes or until golden brown and tender.

3. Add beef broth and Worcestershire sauce to mushroom mixture; bring to boil.

4. In small bowl, mix cornstarch with water to make a smooth paste. Add to pan, whisking until combined and thickened. Season to taste with salt and pepper.

5. Divide rice among 4 plates. Place 2 SPAM® Classic slices on top of rice. Top with gravy and 1 egg. Garnish with parsley, green onion, and tomato, if desired.

SPAM® Breakfast Hash

🕐 **TIME:** 25 MINUTES   🍴 **YIELD:** 4–6 SERVINGS

What could be more classic breakfast than a cast-iron skillet full of browned potatoes, cooked bell peppers, and of course, glorious SPAM® Classic? It's the meal that'll have you asking, "Hash anyone started making breakfast yet?"

INGREDIENTS

- 1 (12-ounce) can SPAM® Classic, diced
- 2 tablespoons canola oil
- 1 finely chopped onion
- 2 large baking potatoes, peeled and diced
- ½ red bell pepper, chopped
- ½ green bell pepper, chopped
- ¼ cup chopped fresh parsley
- ¼ teaspoon freshly ground pepper

DIRECTIONS

1. In 10-inch cast-iron skillet, heat oil over medium heat. Cook onions 3 minutes or until translucent.

2. Add potatoes and cook 7 to 10 minutes or until golden. Stir in SPAM® Classic and red and green bell peppers, and cook until heated through and browned. Stir in chopped parsley and pepper.

SPAM® Breakfast Musubi

🕐 **TIME:** 40 MINUTES   🍴 **YIELD:** 8 SERVINGS

Wake up your taste buds with this breathtaking breakfast musubi. Kick off your day with a meaty helping of protein. The egg and cheese will remind you that this heavenly creation is in fact a breakfast sandwich. The nori and rice will stop you from ever buying a normal fast-food breakfast sandwich again.

INGREDIENTS

- 1 (12-ounce) can SPAM® with Real HORMEL® Bacon, cut into 8 slices
- 4 eggs
- 2 teaspoons Mirin
- 1 teaspoon sugar
- Salt
- 2 teaspoons Dashi (optional)
- 2 teaspoons oil
- 2 sheets Nori, cut into 8 strips
- 3 cups cooked sushi rice
- Furikake
- 4 slices Cheddar cheese, cut in half

DIRECTIONS

1. In large skillet, over medium-high heat, cook SPAM® with Real HORMEL® Bacon slices 3 to 5 minutes or until browned.

2. In medium bowl, whisk together eggs, Mirin, sugar, a pinch of salt and Dashi. In large non-stick skillet over medium heat, heat oil. Pour one-third egg mixture into pan. Once eggs start to set, fold it like an omelet onto itself, turning it to the side of the pan, making room to add another one-third amount of egg mixture. Let that amount set and roll omelet in opposite direction to layer together. Repeat with remaining egg mixture to create one layered rolled omelet. Cut into 8 sections.

3. On top of Nori strip, place ⅓ cup rice into Musubi press, or plastic wrap lined SPAM® can and press down. Remove press. Sprinkle rice with Furikake. Top with halved cheese slice and egg portion. Top with one slice of SPAM® with Real HORMEL® Bacon. Wrap Nori around Musubi, moistening edge of Nori to adhere together. Repeat to make 8.

SPAM® Benedict

🕐 **TIME:** 40 MINUTES   🍴 **YIELD:** 4 SERVINGS

You know who Benedict Arnold was? Some guy who betrayed the USA a long time ago. You know who a SPAM® Benedict Arnold is? Some guy who takes your buttery, toasted SPAM® Benedict English muffins.

INGREDIENTS

- 1 (12-ounce) can SPAM® Classic
- 4 egg yolks
- 3½ tablespoons lemon juice
- 1 tablespoon water
- 1 cup butter, melted
- Salt, to taste
- 1 teaspoon white vinegar
- 8 large eggs
- 4 English muffins, split and toasted
- ½ cup fresh spinach
- 8 slices tomato
- 1 tablespoon chopped chives, if desired

DIRECTIONS

1. To make the Hollandaise sauce, fill the bottom of a double-boiler part-way with water; make sure water does not touch the top of the pan. Bring the water to a simmer. In the top of a double boiler, whisk together egg yolks, lemon juice, and 1 tablespoon water.

2. Add butter to the egg yolk mixture 1 or 2 tablespoons at a time, whisking constantly. If sauce becomes too thick, add 1 to 2 teaspoons hot water. Whisk until butter is incorporated. Whisk in salt; remove from heat. Cover pan.

3. To poach the eggs, fill a large saucepan with 3 inches of water. Bring to a gentle simmer; add vinegar. Carefully break eggs into simmering water; cook 2½ to 3 minutes or until whites are cooked and yolks are still soft in center. Remove eggs from water with a slotted spoon; set on a warm plate.

4. Meanwhile, cut SPAM® Classic into 4 (¼-inch-thick) slices. In medium skillet, heat SPAM® slices over medium-high heat until lightly crisp.

5. Place English muffins, cut-side-up, on serving plates. Top evenly with spinach, SPAM® slices, tomato, and poached egg. Drizzle with Hollandaise sauce. Sprinkle with chives, if desired. Serve immediately.

SPAM® Monkey Bread

🕐 **TIME:** 50 MINUTES   🍴 **YIELD:** 6–8 SERVINGS

This award winning SPAM® recipe has only gotten better, moving from first place to the grand prize winner in only a year! It's sweet and savory, chock full of SPAM® with Real HORMEL® Bacon, butter biscuits, cinnamon, honey, and maple bourbon.

INGREDIENTS

- 1 (12 ounce) can SPAM® with Real HORMEL® Bacon, diced
- 2 (16.3 ounce) cans refrigerated butter-flavored biscuits
- ½ cup sugar
- 1 teaspoon cinnamon
- ¾ cup butter
- 1 cup brown sugar
- 2½ tablespoons maple-flavored bourbon
- 2 tablespoons honey

DIRECTIONS

1. Heat oven to 350°F. Generously spray 10-inch fluted tube pan with non-stick cooking spray.

2. In large skillet over medium heat, cook SPAM® with Real HORMEL® Bacon 3 to 5 minutes, or until crisped and browned.

3. Cut each biscuit into 8 pieces. Combine sugar and cinnamon in large plastic bag. Add biscuit pieces and shake to coat.

4. Layer ⅓ SPAM® with Real HORMEL® Bacon pieces in bottom of prepared pan. Top with half of the biscuit pieces. Layer another ⅓ SPAM® with Real HORMEL® Bacon pieces and the remaining biscuit pieces. Sprinkle the remaining SPAM® with Real HORMEL® Bacon pieces on top.

5. In small saucepan over medium heat, melt butter. Continue to cook, stirring constantly, 1 to 2 minutes or until light brown. Remove from heat. Whisk in brown sugar, bourbon and honey. Pour over biscuit pieces.

6. Bake 30 to 40 minutes, or until biscuit pieces are cooked through and top is browned. Allow bread to cool 5 minutes before turning out onto serving platter. Serve immediately.

Enchilada Breakfast
SPAM® Casserole

 TIME: 60 MINUTES   **YIELD:** 8 SERVINGS

 It's a new dawn of deliciousness. Awake to the taste of enchanting enchiladas made with spicy CHI-CHI'S® Diced Green Chilies and SPAM® Classic.

INGREDIENTS

- 1 (12-ounce) can SPAM® Classic, cut into cubes
- 8 fajita-size flour tortillas
- ½ cup onion
- ½ cup green bell pepper
- 1 tomato, chopped
- 1½ cups shredded Cheddar cheese, divided
- 4 large eggs
- 2 cups whipping cream
- 1 (4.25-ounce) can CHI-CHI'S® Diced Green Chilies
- Picante sauce, for serving

DIRECTIONS

1. In the center of each tortilla, place about ¼ cup SPAM® Classic cubes, 1 tablespoon onion, 1 tablespoon bell pepper, 1 tablespoon tomato, and 1 tablespoon cheese; roll up tightly.

2. In a greased 13 x 9-inch baking dish, place tortilla rolls seam-side-down.

3. In a bowl, beat together eggs, cream, and chilies; pour over enchiladas. Cover; refrigerate overnight.

4. Heat oven to 350°F.

5. Bake casserole 40 to 50 minutes or until egg mixture is set. Sprinkle with remaining 1 cup cheese. Bake 5 minutes longer or until cheese is melted. Serve with picante sauce.

SPAM® Huevos Chilaquiles

TIME: 35 MINUTES   **YIELD:** 6 SERVINGS

 Can breakfast be tasty enough to change the expression "good morning" to "great morning"? It can if it's made with eggs, cheese, SPAM® Classic, and CHI-CHI'S® Thick & Chunky Hot Salsa.

INGREDIENTS

- 1 (12-ounce) can SPAM® Classic, cut into thin strips
- 4 cups corn tortilla chips
- 1 cup CHI-CHI'S® Thick & Chunky Hot Salsa
- 1 cup shredded Chihuahua cheese or Monterey Jack cheese
- 6 eggs

DIRECTIONS

1. In large skillet over medium-high heat, cook SPAM® Classic strips 3 to 5 minutes or until browned and crisped.

2. Heat oven to 350°F. Lightly grease 13×9-inch baking dish.

3. Layer half of the tortilla chips in prepared baking dish. Top with half of the cooked SPAM® Classic strips, half of the salsa and 1 cup of the cheese. Press layers gently down into casserole. Repeat with remaining tortilla chips, SPAM® Classic strips, salsa and cheese.

4. Bake 30 minutes or until cheese is melted and golden brown. Top individual servings with 1 egg.

Huevos SPAM® Cheros

🕐 **TIME:** 15 MINUTES   🍴 **YIELD:** 6 SERVINGS

You are going to want to try these Huevos SPAM® Cheros right away! Seriously, what are you still reading this for? You should be making this recipe already, it's so good! Quit reading this! Go! This is next level SPAM® Classic and eggs! Get to it! The egg timer is already ticking! Hurry!

INGREDIENTS

- 1 (12-ounce) can SPAM® Classic, cut into thin slices
- 2 tablespoons vegetable oil
- 6 (6-inch) corn tortillas
- 2 tablespoons butter
- 6 large eggs
- 2 cups crumbled Queso Fresco cheese
- Salsa, for serving

DIRECTIONS

1. In large skillet over medium-high heat, heat oil. Quickly fry tortillas in hot oil. Drain on paper towel lined tray.

2. In same skillet, melt butter. Fry eggs to desired doneness. Remove from pan.

3. In same skillet, cook SPAM® Classic slices 2 to 3 minutes or until crisped and browned.

4. Divide SPAM® Classic slices among 6 tortillas. Top each with 1 egg. Sprinkle with cheese and top with salsa.

SPAM® Breakfast Burrito

🕐 **TIME:** 30 MINUTES   🍴 **YIELD:** 4 SERVINGS

This delicious start to your day brings together a tasty mix of eggs, black beans, avocado, and more with SPAM® Classic.

INGREDIENTS

- 1 (12-ounce) can SPAM® Classic, cut into cubes
- 4 large burrito-sized tortillas
- 4 eggs, scrambled
- 2 hash brown patties, prepared according to package directions
- 1 cup shredded Cheddar cheese
- 1 cup shredded Monterey Jack cheese
- 1 avocado, peeled, pitted and sliced
- 1 cup cooked black beans
- ½ cup Pico de Gallo

DIRECTIONS

1. In large skillet, over medium-high heat, cook SPAM® Classic 3 to 5 minutes or until browned. Remove from skillet.

2. Fill each tortilla evenly with ingredients. Roll up burritos. in large skillet, over medium heat, place burritos one at a time and cook 1 to 2 minutes, turning to griddle all sides, until toasted and light brown.

SPAM® Bagel Sandwich

 TIME: 15 MINUTES   **YIELD:** 1 SERVING

 Grab your fave bagel and fill it with slices of SPAM® with Real HORMEL® Bacon, an egg, cheese, and fresh toppings. Voila! Your breakfast-on-the-go sandwich is ready.

INGREDIENTS

- 2 slices SPAM® with Real HORMEL® Bacon
- 2 tablespoons butter, softened
- 1 everything bagel, split
- 1 slice American cheese
- 1 fried egg, cooked over easy
- Toppings: arugula leaves, tomato slices, red onion slices

DIRECTIONS

1. Cook SPAM® with Real HORMEL® Bacon according to package directions, until golden.

2. Spread butter over cut sides of bagel. Toast until golden brown.

3. Cover the bottom bagel half with SPAM® with Real HORMEL® Bacon slices, cheese, and egg. Top with desired toppings and the remaining bagel half.

SPAM® Baked French Toast

⏱ **TIME:** 60 MINUTES   🍴 **YIELD:** 12 SERVINGS

This grand-prize winning recipe of the 2018 Great American SPAM® Championship captured the hearts, minds, and most importantly—mouths—of the judges. And although it's French, it has a Hawaiian-style twist, like someone who wears a beret with sandals. So say au revoir to ordinary French toast and say aloha to a simple and delicious recipe that's sure to win you over.

INGREDIENTS

- 1 (12-ounce) can SPAM® with Real HORMEL® Bacon, cubed
- 1 (16-ounce) loaf Hawaiian sliced bread, cubed into 1-inch pieces
- 8 eggs
- 1 cup half-and-half
- 1 cup coconut milk
- 1 cup crushed pineapple, well drained
- ½ cup sweetened flaked coconut, divided

DIRECTIONS

1. Heat oven to 350°F. Lightly grease 9 x 13-inch baking dish.

2. In large skillet over medium heat, cook SPAM® with Real HORMEL® Bacon 2 to 3 minutes or until lightly browned; set aside to cool.

3. Spread bread cubes in prepared pan, sprinkle SPAM® with Real HORMEL® Bacon over top.

4. In large bowl, beat eggs, half-and-half and coconut milk. Stir in crushed pineapple and half of the sweetened flaked coconut. Pour evenly over the SPAM® with Real Hormel® Bacon. Press bread down slightly to absorb the egg mixture.

5. Bake uncovered for 30 minutes. Sprinkle with remaining coconut flakes and bake 15 minutes or until coconut is toasted.

Ultimate SPAM® Breakfast SLT

 TIME: 40 MINUTES   **YIELD:** 8 SERVINGS

 Say B-Y-E to the B-L-T. Nothing against bacon. But another pork product is ready to step in like a delicious stunt double: SPAM® Classic. It does all its own moves like flipping, frying, and topping. The result is an action-packed, flavor-packed breakfast coming soon to a plate near you.

INGREDIENTS

- 1 (12-ounce) can SPAM® Classic, sliced into 8 slices
- 4 Roma tomatoes, halved lengthwise
- 1 tablespoon olive oil
- ¾ teaspoon garlic powder, divided
- ¾ teaspoon salt, divided
- ½ teaspoon pepper, divided
- 2 teaspoons sugar
- 1 tablespoon chopped fresh basil leaves
- ¾ cup mayonnaise
- 1 avocado, pitted, peeled, and mashed
- 8 English muffins, spilt and toasted
- Fresh spinach leaves
- 8 eggs, cooked sunny-side up

DIRECTIONS

1. Heat oven to 450°F. Line rimmed baking sheet with parchment paper. Arrange SPAM® Classic slices on one half of baking sheet.

2. Place Roma tomatoes, cut-side up on other half of baking sheet. Drizzle tomatoes with olive oil, sprinkle with ½ teaspoon garlic powder, ½ teaspoon salt, ¼ teaspoon pepper, sugar, and basil.

3. Bake 25 to 30 minutes or until SPAM® Classic is crisped and browned and tomatoes are softened, turning once during baking.

4. In small bowl, combine mayonnaise, avocado, remaining ¼ teaspoon garlic powder, ¼ teaspoon salt, and ¼ teaspoon pepper until well combined.

5. Spread avocado mixture on split English muffins. Top bottom halves with spinach leaves, 1 SPAM® Classic slice, 1 tomato, 1 egg, and muffin top.

SPAM® Waffle with Cheese

🕐 **TIME:** 30 MINUTES   🍴 **YIELD:** 6 SERVINGS

 Why does anyone eat anything other than waffles? We don't know. And now we've added glorious SPAM® Classic and Cheddar cheese! Sorry, other breakfasts. People may just never go back.

INGREDIENTS

- 1 (12-ounce) can SPAM® Classic
- 2 cups pancake and baking mix
- 1⅓ cups milk
- 2 tablespoons vegetable oil
- 1 egg
- 1 cup shredded Cheddar cheese
- Syrup, as desired

DIRECTIONS

1. Cut SPAM® Classic in half. Shred one half on box grater; reserve. Dice remaining half.
2. In medium skillet over medium-high heat, cook diced SPAM® Classic 3 to 5 minutes or until browned and crisped. Reserve.
4. Heat waffle iron; grease if necessary. In large bowl, stir pancake and baking mix, milk, oil, egg and cheese until blended. Stir in reserved grated SPAM® Classic.
5. Pour about 1 cup batter onto center of hot waffle iron; close lid.
6. Bake 5 minutes or until steaming stops. Carefully remove waffle. Repeat with remaining batter.
7. Top waffles with reserved diced SPAM® Classic. Serve with syrup, as desired.

SPAM® Classic and Spinach Mini Quiches

 TIME: 40 MINUTES   **YIELD:** 15 SERVINGS

 Whip up a delightful breakfast or snack with our quick-and-easy SPAM® Classic and Spinach Mini Quiches. Featuring diced SPAM® Classic, eggs, spinach, and Swiss and Cheddar cheeses, these mini quiches are effortlessly delicious. Encased in flaky buttermilk biscuit dough, these savory bites bake to perfection for a convenient and satisfying treat.

INGREDIENTS

- 1 (12-ounce) can SPAM® Classic, diced
- 8 large eggs, lightly beaten
- ½ (10-ounce) package frozen chopped spinach, thawed and squeezed dry
- ¼ cup minced onion
- ½ cup milk
- ½ cup shredded Swiss cheese
- ½ cup shredded Cheddar cheese
- ¼ teaspoon ground nutmeg
- ⅛ teaspoon pepper
- 3 (12-ounce) cans refrigerated buttermilk biscuit dough

DIRECTIONS

1. Heat oven to 350°F.
2. Grease muffin pans.
3. In a large bowl, combine SPAM® Classic, eggs, spinach, onion, milk, cheeses, nutmeg, and pepper. Mix well.
4. Place biscuits in muffin cups, pressing gently to fit.
5. Spoon the SPAM® Classic filling into each cup.
6. Bake quiches for 25 to 30 minutes until golden brown and egg mixture is set. Serve warm.

SPAM® Maple Flavored Waffle Breakfast Sandwich

 TIME: 30 MINUTES   **YIELD:** 4 SERVINGS

 Satisfy your sweet tooth and your meat tooth! Enjoy slices of sizzling sweet SPAM® Maple Flavored and a fried egg sandwiched between Belgian waffles. Add maple syrup to make it extra sweet.

INGREDIENTS

- 1 (12-ounce) can SPAM® Maple Flavored, cut into 8 slices
- 4 fried eggs
- 8 small frozen Belgian waffles, toasted
- Maple syrup, if desired

DIRECTIONS

1. In large skillet, over medium-high heat, cook SPAM® Maple Flavored slices 3 to 5 minutes or until browned.
2. Assemble sandwiches by dividing eggs among 4 waffles. Layer each with 2 SPAM® Maple Flavored slices and top with remaining waffles.
3. Serve with maple syrup, if desired.

SPAM® Maple Flavored Breakfast Bowl

 TIME: 30 MINUTES   **YIELD:** 4 SERVINGS

 We're not yolking, this breakfast bowl, featuring slices of SPAM® Maple Flavored, sweet potatoes, onions, spinach, and fried eggs, is so easy to make and so delicious you'll want it every morning.

INGREDIENTS

- 1 (12-ounce) can SPAM® Maple Flavored, cut into 8 slices
- 2 tablespoons olive oil
- 2 sweet potatoes, peeled and diced
- 1 onion, diced
- 5 ounces baby spinach leaves
- ½ teaspoon freshly cracked black pepper
- 4 fried eggs, if desired

DIRECTIONS

1. In large skillet, over medium-high heat, cook SPAM® Maple Flavored slices 3 to 5 minutes or until browned. Remove from pan.

2. In same skillet, over medium-high heat, heat oil. Add sweet potatoes. Cook 7 to 10 minutes or until golden brown.

3. Add onions. Cook 3 minutes or until translucent. Stir in spinach, cooking 2 to 3 minutes or until wilted.

4. Season with pepper. Top sweet potato mixture with SPAM® Maple Flavored slices. Serve with eggs, if desired.

SPAM® Western Omelet

  TIME: 25 MINUTES   **YIELD:** 4 SERVINGS

This Western omelet is a sizzling breakfast option. Diced SPAM® Classic, sautéed in butter and chili powder, provides a rich and meaty foundation. As you take a bite, the omelet's fluffy eggs blend harmoniously with the vibrant bell pepper, onions, and a hint of milk, creating a delightful interplay of textures and tastes. The finishing touch of salt and a light sear in vegetable oil adds a savory depth, making each mouthful a satisfying symphony of flavors.

INGREDIENTS

- 2 tablespoons vegetable oil
- 1 chopped large green bell pepper
- 2 thinly sliced medium onions
- 1 (12-ounce) can SPAM® Classic, diced
- ¼ teaspoon chili powder
- 8 large eggs
- 4 tablespoons milk
- ½ teaspoon salt
- Black pepper, to taste
- 4 teaspoons butter or margarine

DIRECTIONS

1. In a medium skillet, heat oil and sauté the bell pepper and onions until lightly browned.
2. Stir in the SPAM® Classic and chili powder until well mixed.
3. For each omelet, in a bowl, beat together 2 eggs, 1 tablespoon milk, ⅛ teaspoon salt, and black pepper.
4. In an 8- or 9-inch omelet pan or skillet, melt 1 teaspoon of butter and pour in the egg mixture.
5. Cook over medium heat, pushing the cooked edge of the omelet to center as the egg sets and tilting pan to allow the uncooked mixture to run to the edge.
6. When the surface of the omelet is set, spoon ½ cup of the SPAM® mixture onto half of the omelet, and then flip the uncovered half over the filling.
7. Cook until the bottom of the omelet is browned. Serve.

Top-of-the-Morning SPAM® Breakfast Bake

 TIME: 1 HOUR   **YIELD:** 10 SERVINGS

 Your morning yawn will turn to "yay!" after one bite of this blue-ribbon-winning comfort food dish. Featuring SPAM® Hickory Smoke Flavored along with a flavorful mix of ingredients, it's one easy and tasty crack-of-dawn creation.

INGREDIENTS

- 2 tablespoons butter
- 1 (12-ounce) can SPAM® Hickory Smoke Flavored, cut into cubes
- ½ cup onion, diced
- 3 cups frozen diced potatoes, thawed
- 1 cup sour cream
- 3 tablespoons ranch seasoning mix
- 1 (10.75-ounce) can cream of mushroom soup
- 2 cups shredded sharp Cheddar cheese
- ¼ cup Italian herbs cooking cream
- 1 (16-ounce) can refrigerated buttermilk biscuit dough

DIRECTIONS

1. Heat oven to 350°F. Grease a 13x9-inch baking dish.

2. In a large skillet, melt the butter over medium-high heat. Add SPAM® Hickory Smoke Flavored and onion; cook, stirring occasionally, for 10 minutes or until golden brown.

3. In a large bowl, combine potatoes, sour cream, ranch seasoning, soup, cheese, and cooking cream.

4. Add the SPAM® mixture and stir to combine. Spoon the mixture into the baking dish.

5. Cut each biscuit into 6 wedges, then place each wedge over the SPAM® mixture with points facing upward.

6. Bake for 25 to 30 minutes or until biscuits are cooked through and golden brown.

SPAM® Maple Flavored Breakfast Poutine

🕐 **TIME:** 30 MINUTES 🍽️ **YIELD:** 4 SERVINGS

For a sweet take on Canadian-snack-time-favorite poutine, we started with French toast sticks, cubes of SPAM® Maple Flavored, syrup, berries, and a sprinkling of powdered sugar. This is one breakfast that is sure to get 3 yums up!

INGREDIENTS

- 1 (12-ounce) can SPAM® Maple Flavored, cubed
- 1 (12- to 16-ounce) package frozen French toast sticks, prepared according to package instructions
- Maple syrup
- Whipped cream
- Berries
- Powdered sugar

DIRECTIONS

1. In large skillet, over medium-high heat, cook SPAM® Maple Flavored cubes 3 to 5 minutes or until browned and crisped.

2. On serving platter, place prepared French toast sticks. Top with browned SPAM® Maple Flavored cubes, maple syrup, whipped cream, berries, and powdered sugar as desired.

SPAMKINS™ Breakfast Muffins

 TIME: 35 MINUTES   **YIELD:** 8 SERVINGS

 Instead of setting your alarm clock, set your mind to make breakfast muffins sprinkled with cinnamon and SPAM® with Real HORMEL® Bacon. If that doesn't wake you up, nothing will.

INGREDIENTS

- 1½ cups all-purpose flour
- 2 (¼-ounce) packages rapid-rise yeast
- 2 tablespoons plus ½ cup sugar, divided
- ½ teaspoon salt
- ⅔ cup plus 2 tablespoons warm milk, divided
- ¼ cup melted butter
- 4 large eggs, divided
- 1 teaspoon ground cinnamon
- 1 (12-ounce) can SPAM® with Real HORMEL® Bacon, diced and sautéed in small amount of butter
- ⅓ cup maple-flavored syrup

DIRECTIONS

1. Lightly coat 18 regular-size muffin cups with cooking spray.

2. Make the batter in a large bowl, combining the flour, yeast, 2 tablespoons sugar, salt, ⅔ cup milk, butter, and 1 egg; mix well.

3. Place about 1 tablespoon of batter into each muffin cup.

4. In a small bowl, combine the remaining ½ cup sugar and the cinnamon; mix well. Divide and sprinkle sugar-cinnamon mixture over muffins.

5. Sprinkle about 1 tablespoon SPAM® with Real HORMEL® Bacon over each muffin.

6. In separate bowl, whisk together the remaining 3 eggs and 2 tablespoons milk. Pour about 1 tablespoon of the egg mixture over each muffin and drizzle them with syrup.

7. Place muffin pans in a cold oven and set the temperature to 350°F. Once the oven reaches the temperature, bake the muffins for 15 to 20 minutes or until the egg mixture is set.

8. Remove pans from the oven and cool the muffins in the pan for 5 minutes.

9. Remove muffins from the pan and serve warm or at room temperature. Serve with additional maple syrup for dipping, if desired.

Spiced Dutch Baby Pancake with SPAM® Figgy Pudding and Cranberry Butter

 TIME: 40 MINUTES   **YIELD:** 4 SERVINGS

Now, bring us some figgy pudding. Now bring us pancakes with SPAM® Figgy Pudding. Now bring us pancakes with SPAM® Figgy Pudding and cranberry butter, and bring it right here! Make it a holiday breakfast they'll never forget with cubes of limited-edition SPAM® Figgy Pudding enveloped in a golden, fluffy Dutch baby pancake and topped with cranberry sauce and powdered sugar.

INGREDIENTS

- 3 eggs
- ½ cup milk
- ½ cup flour
- 1 teaspoon cinnamon
- ⅛ teaspoon nutmeg
- ¼ cup butter
- 1 (12-ounce) can SPAM® Figgy Pudding, cubed and browned*
- ¼ cup softened butter
- 2 tablespoons cranberry sauce
- Powdered sugar, if desired
- Maple syrup, if desired

DIRECTIONS

1. Heat oven to 425°F.

2. In large bowl, beat eggs until frothy. Add milk, flour, cinnamon, and nutmeg. Whisk 2 to 3 minutes or until well combined and batter is smooth.

3. In 10-inch cast iron skillet, over medium-high heat, melt butter. Pour batter into pan and scatter half of the SPAM® Figgy Pudding cubes over the top.

4. Bake 20 to 25 minutes or until puffed and golden. Top with remaining SPAM® Figgy Pudding cubes.

5. In small bowl, combine softened butter and cranberry sauce.

6. Serve with cranberry butter, powdered sugar, and maple syrup, if desired.

Can't get your hands on SPAM® Figgy Pudding? Try this recipe with SPAM® Classic.

SPAM® Sriracha Benedict

⏱ **TIME:** 40 MINUTES   🍴 **YIELD:** 4 SERVINGS

 After one bite, this breakfast classic will have your taste buds asking for seconds . . . and thirds.

INGREDIENTS

- 4 egg yolks
- 3½ tablespoons lemon juice
- 1 tablespoon water
- 1 cup butter, melted
- Salt to taste
- 1 tablespoon sriracha sauce
- 1 teaspoon white vinegar
- 8 large eggs
- 1 (12-ounce) can SPAM® Classic, cut into 8 slices
- 4 English muffins, split and toasted
- 1 avocado, sliced
- 8 slices tomato
- Chopped fresh cilantro, if desired
- Red pepper, if desired

DIRECTIONS

1. To make Hollandaise sauce, fill bottom of double boiler partway with water; make sure water does not touch top pan. Bring water to a simmer.

2. In top of the double boiler, whisk together egg yolks, lemon juice, and 1 tablespoon water.

3. Add butter to egg yolk mixture 1 or 2 tablespoons at a time, whisking constantly. If sauce becomes too thick, add 1 to 2 teaspoons hot water. Whisk until butter is incorporated.

4. Whisk in salt and sriracha; remove from heat and cover.

5. To poach eggs, fill large saucepan with 3 inches of water. Bring water to a gentle simmer, add vinegar.

6. Carefully break eggs into the simmering water and cook 2½ to 3 minutes or until whites are cooked and yolks are still soft in center, then remove the eggs with a slotted spoon and set on warm plate.

7. In a medium skillet, cook SPAM® Classic over medium-high heat 3 to 4 minutes or until lightly crisp.

8. Place English muffins, cut side up, on serving plates. Top evenly with avocado, tomato, SPAM® Classic, and poached egg. Drizzle with Hollandaise sauce. Sprinkle with cilantro and red pepper, if desired. Serve immediately.

SPAM® Frittata

  TIME: 30 MINUTES   **YIELD:** 4 SERVINGS

If you're having trouble waking up your taste buds for breakfast, we suggest this easy morning masterpiece made with hearty potatoes, green bell peppers, and SPAM® Classic.

INGREDIENTS

- 3 tablespoons vegetable oil, divided
- ½ cup onion, coarsely chopped
- ½ cup green bell pepper, coarsely chopped
- 1 (7-ounce) can SPAM® Classic, diced
- 2 medium potatoes, cooked, peeled, and cubed
- 10 pitted ripe olives, chopped
- 6 large eggs
- 2 tablespoons water
- ¼ teaspoon salt
- ¼ teaspoon pepper

DIRECTIONS

1. In a 10-inch omelet pan or skillet, heat 2 tablespoons of oil and sauté the onion and bell pepper until lightly browned.

2. Stir in the SPAM® Classic, potatoes, and olives; cook over low heat, stirring frequently, for 5 minutes.

3. Loosen food from the bottom of the pan. Add the remaining 1 tablespoon oil and tilt the pan to coat the bottom.

4. In a bowl, mix eggs, water, salt, and black pepper, and then pour over the SPAM® brand mixture.

5. Cover and cook over low heat for 15 minutes or until frittata is set on top. With a pancake turner, loosen the edge and bottom, and invert onto serving platter.

SPAM® Classic and Waffle Musubi with Spicy Maple Syrup

 TIME: 45 MINUTES   **YIELD:** 8 SERVINGS

 Enjoy crispy slices of SPAM® Classic nestled in a bed of sushi rice atop a heated waffle, wrapped in nori, and drizzled with spicy maple syrup in every bite of this SPAM® Classic and Waffle Musubi.

INGREDIENTS

- ¼ cup flour
- 2 eggs, beaten
- 1 cup panko breadcrumbs
- 1 (12-ounce) can SPAM® Classic, cut into 8 slices
- Vegetable oil
- 3 cups cooked white sushi rice
- 4 frozen waffles, toasted and cut in half
- 2 sheets nori, cut lengthwise into quarters
- 1 cup pure maple syrup
- 2 tablespoons cayenne pepper hot sauce

DIRECTIONS

1. Place flour, eggs, and breadcrumbs in separate shallow dishes. Dredge SPAM® Classic slices in flour, dip in eggs, and roll in breadcrumbs.

2. In large skillet, pour enough vegetable oil to cover bottom by 1 inch. Heat oil over medium-high heat. Add breaded SPAM® Classic slices to skillet and fry 3 to 5 minutes, turning once, until golden brown. Remove from skillet.

3. With moist hands, mold rice into 8 blocks with same dimensions as SPAM® slices. Place rice blocks on halved waffles. Top with breaded SPAM® Classic slice. Wrap individual nori strips around each middle, moistening edge of nori to fasten it.

4. In small bowl, combine maple syrup and hot sauce. Serve on side or drizzle on top.

APPETIZERS

44 SPAM® Musubi

45 SPAM® Fries

46 SPAM® Classic Kimbap

47 SPAMALICIOUS™ Fiesta Dip

48 Creamy SPAM® with Real HORMEL® Bacon and Pasta Nachos

49 Fried SPAM® ball with Spicy Ranch

50 SPAMALICIOUS™ Jalapeño Cheddar Biscuits

51 Mini SPAM® Nacho Burgers

52 Mini SPAM® Arepas

53 SPAM® Crunchy Nuggets

54 SPAM® Pizza Rolls

55 SPAM® Island Appetizer

56 Adobo Fried Rice SPAM® Musubi Bites

57 Adobo SPAM® Musubi

58 Teriyaki and Takuan SPAM® Musubi

59 SPAM® Summer Rolls

60 Spicy Chili Garlic SPAM® Musubi

61 BBQ SPAM® Musubi

62 SPAM® Guacamole Dip

63 Thai SPAM® Salad Cups

64 Asian Inspired SPAM® Meatballs

65 Bacon-Wrapped SPAM® Bites

66 Inside-Out SPAMTASTIC™ Musubi

67 Smoky Sweet SPAM® Maple Flavored Bites

68 SPAM® Classic Mini Korean Corndogs

69 SPAM® Maple Flavored Baked Brie

70 Spicy SPAM® Bites

71 SPAM® Musubi Crunchy Roll

72 Wonderful SPAM® Wontons

SPAM® Classic Kimbap

SPAM® Musubi

TIME: 15 MINUTES **YIELD:** 2 SERVINGS

Say "aloha" to SPAM® Musubi. This Hawaiian take on surf and turf is sure to be a hit at your next luau! Your taste buds will be so pleased by the delicious flavor that they'll throw on a lei and start dancing the hula.

INGREDIENTS

- 2 slices SPAM® Classic, sliced ⅜ inch thick
- 3 ounces cooked white rice, seasoned with furikake and toasted sesame seeds, if desired
- 1 tablespoon HOUSE OF TSANG® HIBACHI GRILL Sweet Ginger Sesame Sauce or HOUSE OF TSANG® General Tso Sauce
- 1 whole sheet nori

DIRECTIONS

1. In large skillet, cook SPAM® Classic until lightly browned and crisp. Drizzle cooked SPAM® Classic with grill sauce or cooking sauce.

2. Place rice into musubi press or line inside of empty SPAM® Classic can with plastic wrap and place rice in can. Press rice down firmly.

3. Sprinkle with seasoned furikake and toasted sesame seeds, if desired.

4. Place SPAM® Classic on rice in press or in can. Press down firmly.

5. Optional (not as pictured above): Top with remaining rice; press down.

6. Remove SPAM® Classic and rice from musubi press or can.

7. On work surface, cut nori to desired width.

8. Lay nori shiny-side-down; top with pressed SPAM® Classic and rice. Wrap nori around pressed SPAM® Classic and rice. Serve immediately.

SPAM® Fries

🕐 **TIME:** 10 MINUTES 🍴 **YIELD:** 1 SERVING

Today is Fryday! Even if it's Saturday, Sunday, Monday, Tuesday, Wednesday, Thursday, or even Friday. Every day is Fryday with these delicious treats. Delicious fried SPAM® Classic with a hint of sweet ginger sauce are sure to make your day, or your Fryday.

INGREDIENTS

- 1 (12-ounce) can SPAM® Classic
- Peanut oil, for frying
- HOUSE OF TSANG® General Tso Sauce or Sriracha Ketchup, for dipping

DIRECTIONS

1. Heat about 4 inches of oil in heavy pan or fryer to 350°F.
2. Cut SPAM® Classic lengthwise into six slices. Cut each slice into 4 thick matchsticks.
3. Place fries in hot oil (in small batches) and fry until golden brown and crisp (about 3 minutes). Drain on paper towels. Serve warm fries with dipping sauces.

SPAM® Classic Kimbap

⏱ **TIME:** 45 MINUTES 🍴 **YIELD:** 4 SERVINGS

 This kimbap is the kim-best. Julienned SPAM® Classic, cucumber, carrots, and sautéed spinach are rolled up in nori for a Korean recipe that's kim-bursting with flavor. As a quick and easy lunch or snack, you can't beat the 'bap.

INGREDIENTS

- 3 cups cooked sushi rice
- 8 sheets nori
- 1 (12-ounce) can SPAM® Classic, julienned and sautéed
- 1 carrot, julienned
- 1 cucumber, thinly sliced into long strips
- 2 eggs, lightly beaten, fried and cut into strips
- 4 cups baby spinach, sautéed and seasoned
- 8 strips yellow pickled radish

DIRECTIONS

1. Place one sheet nori on work surface. With moist hands, spread rice evenly over nori, leaving a 1-inch strip uncovered on one end.
2. Layer SPAM® Classic strips, carrots, cucumber, egg strips, spinach, and pickled radish; roll up.
3. Moisten end of nori with small amount of water to fasten together.
4. Repeat with remaining ingredients.
5. Slice rolls into bite-sized pieces.

SPAMALICIOUS™ Fiesta Dip

 TIME: 20 MINUTES **YIELD:** 16–20 SERVINGS

 SPAM® Jalapeño is throwing a fiesta and you're invited! Bring all your friends and all your chips because this dip makes plenty to go around. Even the party piñata will want to grab a chip and dig in for some spicy flavor.

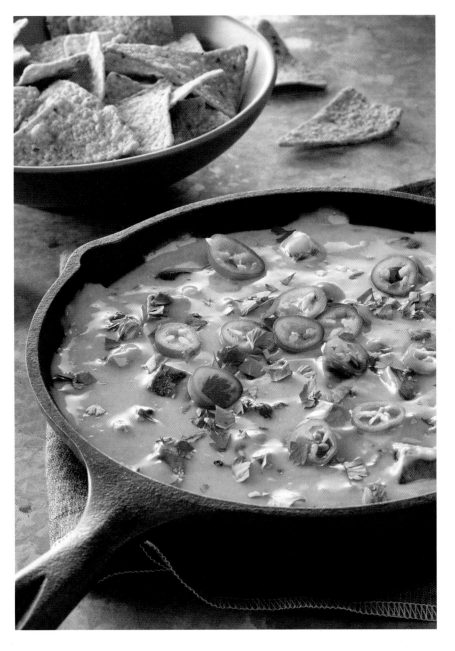

INGREDIENTS

- 1 (12-ounce) can SPAM® Jalapeño, cubed
- 1 (10-ounce) can diced tomatoes with green chilies
- 2 (8-ounce) packages cream cheese
- ½ cup sour cream
- 1 (15-ounce) can of corn, drained
- Tortilla chips, for dipping

DIRECTIONS

1. In a 3-quart saucepan, sauté SPAM® Jalapeño until lightly browned.
2. Add diced tomatoes with green chilies, cream cheese, sour cream, and corn. Stir until cream cheese is melted and dip is warm.
3. Serve with tortilla chips for dipping.

Creamy SPAM® with Real HORMEL® Bacon and Pasta Nachos

🕐 **TIME:** 45 MINUTES 🍴 **YIELD:** 8 SERVINGS

 This recipe brings everyone together! Pasta fans and nacho fans. SPAM® with Real HORMEL® Bacon fans and SPAM® Oven Roasted Turkey fans. Sun-dried red tomato fans and green onion fans. World peace must be just around the corner.

INGREDIENTS

- 1 (12-ounce) can SPAM® with Real HORMEL® Bacon, cut into cubes
- 1 (12-ounce) can SPAM® Oven Roasted Turkey, julienned
- 5 tablespoons packed brown sugar
- 30 to 40 wonton wrappers
- 1 (16-ounce) jar Alfredo sauce, divided
- 2 cups cooked elbow macaroni
- 1½ cups shredded mozzarella cheese
- ¾ cup shredded Parmesan cheese
- ½ cup chopped sun-dried tomatoes
- ¼ cup sliced green onions
- Vegetable oil, for frying

DIRECTIONS

1. Heat oven to 200°F.
2. In large skillet, combine SPAM® with Real HORMEL® Bacon and SPAM® Oven Roasted Turkey; sprinkle each with brown sugar. Cook SPAM® pieces over medium heat until golden brown.
3. Cut wonton wrappers diagonally in half, making triangles. Cook wontons in hot oil until crisp and lightly browned; drain well on paper towels. Transfer fried wontons to baking sheets; place in oven.
4. Meanwhile, in saucepan, heat Alfredo sauce. In large bowl, stir together 1 cup warm Alfredo sauce and the macaroni.
5. Top wontons with SPAM® mixture, macaroni, cheeses and sun-dried tomatoes. Drizzle with remaining Alfredo sauce. Return nachos to oven; heat 5 minutes or until cheese is melted. Top nachos with onions. Serve immediately.

Fried SPAM®ball with Spicy Ranch

 TIME: 30 MINUTES   **YIELD:** VARIES

 "Great balls of fire" isn't just a catchy phrase, it's a way to describe these delicious SPAM®balls. They are most certainly great, as they include sushi rice and mozzarella cheese—and they also have a little fire to them with cayenne pepper in a spicy ranch drizzle. Goodness gracious, these are good.

INGREDIENTS

- 1 cup diced SPAM® Classic
- 2 cups cooked sushi grade rice
- 1 cup shredded mozzarella cheese
- ½ cup chopped parsley
- ½ cup shredded nori
- ½ cup nori powder
- 1 tablespoon gochujang (Korean pepper paste)
- 1 teaspoon cayenne pepper
- 1 teaspoon garlic powder
- 1 tablespoon sesame seeds
- 1 tablespoon sesame oil
- 1 egg
- Salt and pepper to taste
- 2 cups panko breadcrumbs

DIRECTIONS

1. Heat frying oil to 360°F.
2. In a large bowl, add all the ingredients except breadcrumbs and mix them well.
3. Using hands, roll mixture in a 1½-inch rice balls.
4. On large plate, spread panko crumbs and 2 tablespoons chopped parsley and mix well.
5. Roll rice balls in panko crumbs.
6. Deep fry rice balls until golden brown.
7. Place on paper towel lined plate to cool.
8. Place the cooled rice ball on a plate and garnish with spicy ranch and nori powder.

SPAMALICIOUS™ Jalapeño Cheddar Biscuits

 TIME: 35 MINUTES   **YIELD:** 10 SERVINGS

 Imagine the tastiest, savoriest biscuit you can. Then add Cheddar cheese. Now add jalapeños. Now add SPAM® with Real HORMEL® Bacon. Sounds like a SPAMALICIOUS™ recipe, no? It's no daydream. These SPAMALICIOUS™ Jalapeño Cheddar Biscuits add some spice to your breakfast or dinner, in summer or winter.

INGREDIENTS

- ½ cup SPAM® with Real HORMEL® Bacon, diced
- 1 cup plus 1 tablespoon all-purpose flour
- 1 tablespoon plus 2 teaspoons baking powder
- 1 cup plus 1 tablespoon bread flour
- 1 tablespoon sugar
- ¼ teaspoon salt
- ¾ cup milk
- ½ cup shortening or butter
- ½ cup shredded sharp Cheddar cheese
- 1 jalapeño pepper, seeded and diced
- 1 egg, lightly beaten with ½ teaspoon of water

DIRECTIONS

1. Heat oven to 425°F. Line baking sheet with parchment paper.

2. In small skillet over medium-high heat, cook SPAM® with Real HORMEL® Bacon 3 to 5 minutes until lightly browned.

3. In large bowl, mix flours, baking powder, sugar, and salt. Cut in shortening until crumbly. Add milk. Mix until soft dough is formed. Add SPAM® with Real HORMEL® Bacon, cheese and jalapeño; mix just until combined.

4. Turn dough out on a lightly floured work surface. Roll dough out to 1-inch thickness. Cut biscuits with a 2½-inch cutter.

5. Place biscuits ½ inch apart on baking sheet. Brush with beaten egg mixture.

6. Bake biscuits 15 minutes or until golden brown.

Mini SPAM® Nacho Burgers

 TIME: 15 MINUTES   **YIELD:** 6 SERVINGS

 We found a way to hop on the whole mini-burger craze in a big way. With tasty salsa, jalapeño, and guac-topped SPAM® Classic.

INGREDIENTS

- 3 Roma tomatoes, diced
- 3 tablespoons diced red onion
- 3 tablespoons red wine vinegar
- 2 teaspoons minced EMBASA® Chipotle Peppers in Adobo Sauce
- 2 teaspoons honey
- 1 (12-ounce) can SPAM® Classic, cut into 6 slices
- 3 slices Cheddar cheese, cut in half
- 6 small rolls, split and lightly toasted
- 1 cup WHOLLY® Classic Guacamole
- 6 slices CHI-CHI'S® Green Jalapeño Wheels

DIRECTIONS

1. To make salsa, in bowl, stir together tomatoes, onion, vinegar, chipotle peppers in adobo sauce, and honey.

2. Grill or cook SPAM® Classic until lightly browned on both sides. Top SPAM® Classic with cheese; heat until cheese begins to melt.

3. Place 1 slice SPAM® Classic on bottom half of each roll. Top each burger with guacamole, salsa and jalapeño slice. Cover with tops of rolls.

Mini SPAM® Arepas

🕐 **TIME:** 30 MINUTES   🍽 **YIELD:** 8 SERVINGS

Make some mini arepas with major flavor. Cook up soft corn flour patties golden brown on the griddle. Then top them with a mouthwatering mix of SPAM® Classic, diced tomatoes and scrambled egg. That's how you make an easy maize dish taste simply amazing.

INGREDIENTS

- 2 cups Masarepa (pre-cooked corn flour)
- 2 teaspoons salt
- 1½–2 cups warm water
- Oil for pan frying
- 1 (12-ounce) can SPAM® Classic, finely chopped
- 1 (14.5-ounce) can petite diced tomatoes, drained
- 4 eggs, scrambled
- 1 avocado, pitted, peeled, and sliced
- ½ cup crumbled queso fresco

DIRECTIONS

1. In large bowl, combine corn flour and salt. Stir in enough water to form a soft dough. Divide dough into 8 balls; flatten into patties about 3½ inches wide.

2. On greased griddle, place patties; cook over medium heat 3 to 5 minutes or until browned on bottom. Turn and brown other side.

3. In large skillet over medium-high heat, cook SPAM® Classic 3 to 5 minutes or until browned. Stir in tomatoes and cook 2 to 3 minutes or until heated through.

4. Top each arepa with SPAM® Classic mixture, eggs, avocado, and queso fresco.

SPAM® Crunchy Nuggets

⏱ **TIME:** 30 MINUTES   🍴 **YIELD:** 4–8 SERVINGS

 This prize-winning recipe came from Alex Martin-Fonseca (age 7) at the Great American SPAM® Championship. It received 1st Place in 2017 at the Allentown Fair and was the 2018 Grand-Prize winner.

INGREDIENTS

- 1 (12-ounce) can SPAM® Classic
- 6 cups sweetened corn and oat cereal
- 1 cup flour
- 4 eggs, beaten
- ⅓ cup milk
- Maple syrup, for dipping

DIRECTIONS

1. Preheat oven to 350°F. Cut the SPAM® Classic into 16 equal-size pieces; set aside.
2. Crush cereal to resemble bread crumbs; place in bowl. Place flour in a second bowl. In a third bowl, whisk together the eggs and milk.
3. Dip each SPAM® piece into the flour, then egg/milk mixture. Repeat one time, then generously coat each in cereal. Place on baking sheet.
4. Bake 20 minutes or until golden and crisp. Turn pieces about half way through. Serve with maple syrup or your favorite dipping sauce.

SPAM® Pizza Rolls

 TIME: 45 MINUTES   **YIELD:** 6–8 SERVINGS

 Only a genius could create this award winning recipe—and she was only 8 years old! SPAM® Pizza Rolls combine two of the tastiest foods ever: SPAM® Classic and Pizza Rolls.

INGREDIENTS

- ½ teaspoon garlic powder
- 2 tablespoons grated Parmesan cheese
- ½ teaspoon dried Italian seasoning
- ¼ cup olive oil (plus more for brushing dough)
- 1 (11-ounce) can refrigerated pizza crust (thin style)
- 1 (12-ounce) can SPAM® Classic
- 1 (8-ounce) package finely shredded mozzarella cheese
- Pizza sauce, for dipping

DIRECTIONS

1. Heat oven to 400°F. In small bowl, combine garlic powder, Parmesan cheese, Italian seasoning, and olive oil. Set aside.

2. Line a rimmed baking sheet with foil; lightly grease with cooking spray. Remove pizza dough from can; unroll onto the foil. With a small knife, cut dough into 3 long strips. Brush top of the strips lightly with olive oil.

3. Slice the SPAM® Classic into ¼-inch slices then slice in half again lengthwise. Lay the SPAM® slices into two rows down the length of each dough strip. Sprinkle ⅓ of the cheese over each dough strip.

4. Starting at the long end, roll each dough strip until it forms a long log. Finish rolling so that the seam is down. Lightly brush the logs with olive oil.

5. Bake until light brown, about 12 minutes. Brush the tops generously with garlic mixture. Return to oven for another 5 to 8 minutes or until golden brown.

6. Let cool for 10 minutes. Transfer pizza rolls to a cutting board. Slice into 1½-inch pieces. Serve immediately with pizza sauce for dipping.

SPAM® Island Appetizer

TIME: 8 HOURS, 25 MINUTES **YIELD:** 12–16 SERVINGS

Have you ever had an appetizer so great, that you wished it was the main course? Well, prepare yourself for just that. This app is held together by crescent rolls, filled with cream cheese and pineapple, and finally topped SPAM® Classic rubbed in jerk seasoning.

INGREDIENTS

FOR CRUST
- 2 (8-ounce) cans refrigerated crescent roll dough

FOR FILLING
- 1 (8-ounce) package cream cheese, softened
- ⅔ cup mayonnaise
- ½ (8-ounce) can crushed pineapple, drained well
- 4 chopped green onions
- Zest of 1 lime

TOPPING 1
- 1 bunch green onions, chopped
- 1 (15-ounce) can black beans, drained and rinsed
- 1 red bell pepper, seeded and chopped
- 1 (2.25-ounce) can sliced ripe olives
- 2 tablespoons olive oil
- 2 tablespoons lime juice
- 1 garlic clove, minced
- ¼ teaspoon each salt, ground cumin and crushed red pepper flakes
- ⅛ teaspoon ground white pepper

TOPPING 2
- 1 (12-ounce) can SPAM® Classic, finely chopped
- 2–3 teaspoons jerk seasoning blend

TOPPING 3
- 1 cup shredded Cheddar cheese

DIRECTIONS

1. Place unrolled crescent roll dough into a 10 x 15-inch jellyroll pan.
2. Bake at 400°F for 10 minutes or until golden brown. Cool.
3. In bowl, combine filling ingredients; cover and chill until ready to use. In another bowl, combine the ingredients for Topping 1; cover and refrigerate several hours or overnight.
4. In large skillet, sauté SPAM® pieces with jerk seasoning, until crisp and golden brown.
5. At serving time, top crust with the cream cheese filling, followed by the black bean salsa (Topping 1), sautéed SPAM® Classic and the cheese.
6. Cut into squares or triangles and serve.

Adobo Fried Rice
SPAM® Musubi Bites

 TIME: 30 MINUTES   **YIELD:** 8 SERVINGS

For the chef in your life who seemingly has every musubi recipe, here is one they won't have in their collection. A delicious SPAM® Musubi seasoned with Adobo. It's the perfect gift for the seasoned chef—or for anyone with taste buds, really.

INGREDIENTS

- 1 (12-ounce) can SPAM® Less Sodium, cut lengthwise julienne (thin slice)
- 3 cups cooked sushi rice
- 4 sheets Japanese nori, cut in half
- ¼ cup apple cider vinegar
- ¼ cup white vinegar
- 2 tablespoons water
- 2 cloves garlic, chopped
- ¼ cup chopped onion
- 1 bay leaf
- ½ teaspoon cracked black pepper
- 2 tablespoons spy sauce
- 2 tablespoons oyster sauce
- 2 tablespoons brown sugar
- ¼ cup slices green onion
- 2 eggs, scrambled

DIRECTIONS

1. In large skillet, over medium-high heat, cook SPAM® Less Sodium 2 to 3 minutes or until golden brown. Add onions and garlic; cook 1 to 2 minutes or until onions are tender.

2. Add apple cider vinegar, white vinegar, water, bay leaf and black pepper to pan. Reduce heat. Simmer 1 to 2 minutes, or until liquid begins to reduce. Add soy sauce, oyster sauce and brown sugar. Cook 1 to 2 minutes or until mixture is thickened.

3. Add green onions, eggs and cooked rice. Stir-fry 1 to 2 minutes, or until well combined and heated through. Remove from heat. Remove bay leaf.

4. Place ½ cup rice mixture into musubi press, or plastic wrap lined SPAM® can and press down. Remove from press on top of halved nori sheet. Wrap nori around musubi, moistening edge of nori to adhere together. Repeat to make 8. Cut each into bite sized pieces.

Adobo SPAM® Musubi

TIME: 4 HOURS, 10 MINUTES **YIELD:** 8 SERVINGS

Have you heard that we love SPAM® Musubi? WE LOVE SPAM® MUSUBI! Phew, now that you know, try this peppery twist on our classic musubi favorite, adobo-style!

INGREDIENTS

- 1 (12-ounce) can SPAM® Classic, cut into 8 slices
- ¼ cup apple cider vinegar
- ¼ cup mirin or rice vinegar
- ¼ cup water
- 2 cloves garlic, chopped
- 2 green onion whites, cut in half lengthwise
- 2 bay leaves, cracked
- 2 teaspoons black peppercorn, crushed
- 2 teaspoons olive oil
- 3 cups cooked sushi rice
- 4 sheets nori, cut in half

DIRECTIONS

1. In medium bowl, place SPAM® Classic slices. Add cider vinegar, mirin, water, garlic, onion, bay leaves, and peppercorn. Let marinate 1 hour. Remove SPAM® Classic slices from marinade. Reserve marinade.

2. In large skillet over medium high heat, heat oil. Cook SPAM® Classic 2 to 3 minutes or until browned. Add marinade to pan with SPAM® Classic slices; simmer 3 to 4 minutes or until sauce becomes lightly sticky.

3. Place ⅓ cup rice into musubi press or plastic lined SPAM® Classic can on top of halved nori sheet and press down. Top with SPAM® Classic slice. Remove press.

4. Wrap nori around each. Moisten one end slightly to fasten together. Repeat to make 8.

Teriyaki and Takuan SPAM® Musubi

  TIME: 35 MINUTES   **YIELD:** 8 SERVINGS

 The letter of the day is "T." "T" is for "Teriyaki." "T" is for "Takuan." And "T" is for "Tasty"! All three of those T's describe the Teriyaki and Takuan SPAM® Musubi. Just be careful not to drool on your T-shirt.

INGREDIENTS

- 1 (12-ounce) can SPAM® Teriyaki, cut into 8 slices
- 2 tablespoons olive oil
- ¼ cup soy sauce
- ¼ cup water
- 2 tablespoons brown sugar
- 1 tablespoon fresh ginger root juice
- 3 green onion whites, cut in half lengthwise
- 3 cups white cooked sushi rice
- 4 sheets Japanese nori, cut in half
- 1 cup chopped or sliced takuan (pickled daikon)

DIRECTIONS

1. In large skillet over medium-high heat, heat oil. Add SPAM® Teriyaki; cook 2 to 3 minutes or until browned. Remove from pan.

2. In same skillet over medium heat add soy sauce, water, brown sugar, ginger juice, and green onion; reduce heat to simmer. Add SPAM® Teriyaki back to pan; simmer in sauce 3 to 4 minutes or until glazed.

3. Place ⅓ cup rice into musubi press or plastic lined SPAM® Teriyaki can on top of halved nori sheet and press down. Top with SPAM® Teriyaki slice. Remove press.

4. Wrap nori around each. Moisten one end slightly to fasten together. Repeat to make 8.

5. Serve with takuan (pickled daikon). Serve warm.

SPAM® Summer Rolls

⏱ **TIME:** 45 MINUTES　　🍴 **YIELD:** 8 SERVINGS

 If you're a spring roll fan, it's time to take the summer model out for a spin. Make yours with thinly sliced SPAM® Classic strips, rice noodles, cucumber, and carrot folded and rolled. Everything wraps up with a refreshingly sweet and creamy dipping sauce.

INGREDIENTS

- 2 tablespoons soy sauce
- 2 tablespoons sugar
- 1 (12-ounce) can SPAM® Classic, cut into thin strips
- 3 ounces maifun rice stick noodles (angel hair-style)
- 8 (8-inch) round spring roll rice paper wrappers
- ½ cucumber, julienned
- 1 carrot, julienned
- 4 leaves Bibb lettuce, spines removed to make 8 half leaves
- Chopped peanuts
- Lime wedges

PEANUT DIPPING SAUCE

- ¾ cup SKIPPY® Creamy Peanut Butter
- ¼ cup rice vinegar
- ⅓ cup soy sauce
- 3 tablespoons honey
- 1½ teaspoons grated fresh ginger
- 1 clove garlic, minced
- ¼ teaspoon red pepper flakes
- 2 tablespoons water

DIRECTIONS

1. In small bowl, combine soy sauce and sugar.
2. In large skillet over medium-high heat, cook SPAM® Classic strips 3 to 5 minutes or until browned. Add soy sauce sugar mixture, cook 1 to 2 minutes or until slices are glazed. Remove from heat.
3. In pot of boiling water, cook rice stick noodles 2 to 3 minutes or until tender but firm. Rinse under cold running water; drain well.
4. To assemble, pour 1 inch of hot water into 10-inch glass pie plate. Place 1 rice wrapper in water. Let stand 2 to 3 seconds or just until pliable. Place rice wrapper on flat surface. Layer bottom third of wrapper with SPAM® Classic, rice noodles, cucumber, and carrot. Fold 1 piece lettuce in half; place on top. Fold bottom of wrapper up over ingredients. Fold in sides, then continue rolling up. Place seam-side-down on plate. Cover with damp paper towel to keep from drying. Repeat with remaining rice wrappers and filling ingredients.
5. To make dipping sauce, whisk together ingredients. Cut spring rolls in half; serve with dipping sauce.

Spicy Chili Garlic SPAM® Musubi

 TIME: 30 MINUTES   **YIELD:** 4 SERVINGS

 For the musubi fan who has everything, here's a twist that takes things up a notch. It's hot. It's spicy. It's SPAM® Hot & Spicy, made with minced garlic and chili paste. One bite, and you may never go back to plain old musubi.

INGREDIENTS

- 1 (12-ounce) can SPAM® Hot & Spicy, cut lengthwise into 8 slices
- 1 teaspoon olive oil
- 2 tablespoons minced garlic
- 2 tablespoons Sambal chili paste
- 2 tablespoons water
- 1½ teaspoons honey
- ½ teaspoon black pepper
- 3 cups cooked white rice
- 4 sheets nori, cut in half

DIRECTIONS

1. In large skillet over medium-high heat, cook SPAM® slices 3 to 5 minutes or until browned. Remove from skillet.

2. In same skillet, over medium heat, add olive oil and garlic. Sauté 1 to 2 minutes or until garlic is fragrant. Add chili paste, water and honey. Stir to combine. Add SPAM® slices back to the skillet. Cook 2 to 3 minutes or until sauce coats SPAM® slices. Sprinkle with black pepper. Remove from heat.

3. With moist hands, mold rice into 16 blocks the same dimensions as SPAM® slices. Place SPAM® slices on rice blocks and top with another rice block. Wrap each with half sheet of nori, moistening edge of nori to adhere together. Slice each musubi in thirds. Serve with additional chili paste, if desired.

BBQ SPAM® Musubi

⏱ **TIME:** 20 MINUTES   🍽 **YIELD:** 8 SERVINGS

 What is the best kind of party to throw, barbecue or Hawaiian? Trick question! The best kind of party is a Hawaiian barbecue! And we have the perfect main dish—BBQ SPAM® Musubi. So go throw a party and invite all your friends! Their taste buds will thank you.

INGREDIENTS

- 1 ounce olive oil
- 1 (12-ounce) can SPAM® Classic, cut into 8 slices
- 1 ounce water
- ½ cup barbeque sauce
- 4.5 ounces cooked sushi rice
- 4 sheets Japanese nori, cut in half

DIRECTIONS

1. In large skillet over medium high heat, heat oil. Cook SPAM® Classic 2 to 3 minutes or until browned. Add water and BBQ sauce. Cook 2 to 3 minutes or until sauce reduces and becomes a glaze consistency.

2. Place ⅓ cup rice into musubi press or plastic lined SPAM® Classic can on top of halved nori sheet and press down. Top with SPAM® Classic slice. Remove press.

3. Wrap nori around each. Moisten one end slightly to fasten together. Repeat to make 8.

SPAM® Guacamole Dip

 TIME: 5 MINUTES   **YIELD:** 4 SERVINGS

 In our humble opinion, the avocado is neither a fruit nor a vegetable. It's both, something we call a fregetable. To make this easy recipe, use fresh, ripe avocados to make guacamole. Then combine that guacamole with SPAM® Classic for a meaty dip that's absolutely fregetablicious.

INGREDIENTS

- 1 medium avocado, peeled and pitted
- 1 tablespoon lemon juice
- 1 tablespoon chopped onion
- 1 clove of garlic, minced
- ¼ teaspoon salt
- 1 pinch black pepper
- ½ teaspoon hot pepper sauce
- 1 (12-ounce) can SPAM® Classic, finely chopped
- 1 small tomato, chopped
- Crackers or chips, for serving

DIRECTIONS

1. In medium bowl, mash avocado. Add remaining ingredients. Stir to combine.
2. Cover and refrigerate until serving. Serve with crackers or chips.

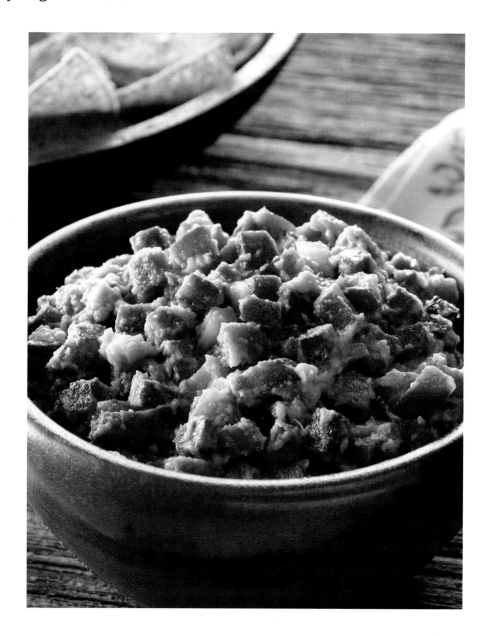

Thai SPAM® Salad Cups

 TIME: 15 MINUTES   **YIELD:** 4 SERVINGS

 Enjoy a salad that's both exotic and hypnotic, a mesmerizing mix of spices and savory SPAM® Classic.

INGREDIENTS

- 2 tablespoons gingerroot, peeled and minced
- 3 cloves garlic, minced
- 1 teaspoon extra-virgin olive oil
- 1 (12-ounce) can SPAM® Classic, cut into cubes
- ¼ cup finely chopped fresh mint
- 1 tablespoon lime juice
- 1 tablespoon sesame seeds, toasted
- ½ teaspoon crushed red pepper flakes
- 4 cups mixed salad greens

DIRECTIONS

1. In skillet, sauté gingerroot and garlic in oil 2 minutes. Add SPAM® Classic; sauté 4 minutes longer.

2. Stir mint, lime juice, sesame seeds and red pepper flakes into skillet; sauté 30 seconds. Spoon mixture over salad greens.

Asian Inspired SPAM® Meatballs

 TIME: 45 MINUTES   **YIELD:** 8 SERVINGS

 Quick to prepare and bursting with flavor, these SPAM® meatballs are destined to be the star of your party spread. Each bite contains a blend of savory SPAM® Classic, vibrant green onions, crisp bean sprouts, and a medley of aromatic spices. Serve them as appetizers or alongside your favorite party dishes, and watch as your guests savor the unique combination of textures and tastes.

INGREDIENTS

- 1 (12-ounce) can SPAM® Classic
- ⅔ cup dry breadcrumbs
- ½ cup bean sprouts, chopped and well drained
- ¼ cup plus ⅓ cup chopped green onions, divided
- ½ teaspoon ground ginger, divided
- ¼ teaspoon black pepper
- ¼ cup green bell pepper, finely chopped
- ½ cup tomato juice

DIRECTIONS

1. Heat oven to 425°F.
2. In a food processor bowl, process the SPAM® Classic until finely chopped or grind by hand.
3. In a bowl, combine the SPAM® Classic, breadcrumbs, bean sprouts, ¼ cup onions, ¼ teaspoon ginger, and black pepper; mix together well.
4. Using about 1 tablespoon for each meatball, shape the mixture into 24 balls.
5. Place on a wire rack in a shallow baking pan and bake for 15 minutes; then cool to room temperature.
6. To make the sauce, use a small saucepan and combine the tomato juice, bell pepper, remaining ⅓ cup onions, and ¼ teaspoon ginger.
7. Bring to a boil and simmer for 5 minutes.
8. Spear the meatballs on cocktail picks. Serve with warm sauce for dipping.

Bacon-Wrapped SPAM® Bites

 TIME: 35 MINUTES   **YIELD:** 16 SERVINGS

 Savor the sizzling meaty synergy of our Bacon-Wrapped SPAM® Bites. Tender SPAM® Classic cubes enveloped in the rich, smoky embrace of HORMEL® BLACK LABEL® Bacon, glazed with a sweet and tangy apple juice and honey mustard fusion, and crowned with a caramelized brown sugar crust. It's the ultimate meat-lover's dream.

INGREDIENTS

- 1 package HORMEL® BLACK LABEL® Bacon
- 1 (12-ounce) can SPAM® Classic, cut into 32 cubes
- ½ cup honey mustard
- ¼ cup packed brown sugar
- 2 tablespoons apple juice

DIRECTIONS

1. Heat oven to 400°F.
2. Partially cook the bacon and drain on paper towel. Cut each slice bacon in half.
3. Wrap the bacon around each cube of SPAM® Classic and secure with a wooden toothpick.
4. Place the SPAM® bites in a 13x9-inch baking dish.
5. In a bowl, combine the mustard, brown sugar, and apple juice, mixing well.
6. Drizzle the mustard mixture over the bacon-wrapped SPAM® Classic.
7. Bake 15 to 20 minutes or until bacon is crisp.

Inside-Out SPAMTASTIC™ Musubi

TIME: 1 HOUR   **YIELD:** 6 SERVINGS

Wrapped in egg in place of the usual nori, this inside-out SPAM® musubi features a Thai peanut sauce drizzled over bacon, SPAM® Classic, sushi rice, and nori.

INGREDIENTS

- 1 (12-ounce) can SPAM® Classic, sliced into ¼-inch slices
- 9 eggs, beaten
- 3 cups cooked sushi rice
- Snack-size nori sheets, broken in pieces
- 6 strips cooked HORMEL® BLACK LABEL® Bacon, cut in half

THAI PEANUT SAUCE

- 1 (13.5-ounce) can of coconut milk
- ¾ cup SKIPPY® Natural Creamy Peanut Butter Spread with Honey
- ¾ cup water
- 6 tablespoons red curry paste
- 2 tablespoons cider vinegar
- 2 teaspoons dark soy sauce
- 1 teaspoon salt

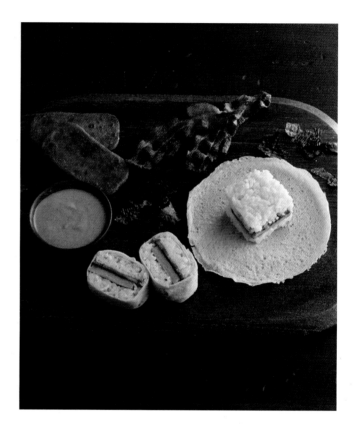

DIRECTIONS

1. In an 8-inch nonstick pan over medium-high heat, cook SPAM® Classic slices 3 to 4 minutes or until browned. Remove from pan.

2. In same skillet, add 3 tablespoons beaten egg, swirling pan to create a thin 8-inch egg sheet. Cook 1 minute or until edges start to pull away from pan. Flip to cook other side 10 seconds. Repeat with remaining eggs to make 12 sheets.

3. To make Thai peanut sauce, combine ingredients in medium saucepan over medium heat. Cook, stirring, 5 to 6 minutes or until heated and smooth.

4. On work surface, place musubi press. Add ½ inch rice to bottom. Top with SPAM® Classic slice. Top with nori pieces, as desired. Spoon small amount of Thai peanut sauce over nori. Top with a half slice of bacon. Cover with another ½ inch rice. Use press to hold musubi down and pull mold upward to unmold the musubi. Cut in half. Repeat with remaining ingredients.

5. Wrap each half in 1 egg wrap. Use extra sauce for dipping.

Smoky Sweet
SPAM® Maple Flavored Bites

 TIME: 45 MINUTES   **YIELD:** 12 SERVINGS

 Smoky Sweet SPAM® Maple Flavored Bites are a harmonious blend of sweet, smoky, and savory that will leave you craving more. Featuring the irresistible SPAM® Maple Flavored, each bite has a harmonious blend of sweet potato, fried capers, and a delicate malt vinegar mousse, all finished with a drizzle of hot honey.

INGREDIENTS

- 1 large sweet potato, peeled and sliced into ½-inch slices
- 1 (12-ounce) can SPAM® Maple Flavored, sliced lengthwise into 6 thick slices, cut in half to make 12 pieces
- 2 tablespoons oil, divided
- 1 tablespoon cane sugar

FRIED CAPERS

- 1 cup oil for frying
- 1 egg, lightly beaten
- 2 tablespoons milk
- 3 dashes hot sauce
- ½ cup flour
- ¼ cup capers, drained and patted dry

MALT VINEGAR MOUSSE

- ½ cup heavy cream
- ¼ cup malt vinegar, preferably smoked

GARNISH

- Hot honey
- Chopped parsley, if desired

DIRECTIONS

1. For the fried capers, in small saucepan, heat oil to 350°F. In shallow bowl, combine egg, milk, and hot sauce. Place flour in separate shallow bowl.

2. Toss capers in flour. Remove to egg mixture to coat. Return to flour to coat again. Fry capers 1 to 2 minutes or until golden brown. Remove to paper-towel-lined plate. Reserve.

3. Using a 1¾-inch biscuit cutter, cut sweet potato slices and SPAM® Maple Flavored pieces into matching shapes.

4. In large skillet over medium-high heat, heat 1 tablespoon oil. Sear sweet potato rounds on each side. Reduce heat. Add sugar and 2 tablespoons water. Allow to cook 3 to 5 minutes, or until tender and glazed.

5. In another skillet over medium-high heat, heat remaining oil. Cook SPAM® Maple Flavored rounds 2 to 3 minutes, turning over, until browned.

6. To make the malt vinegar mousse, in bowl using electric mixer, beat cream until stiff peaks form. Stir in vinegar.

7. Place sweet potatoes on serving dish, top each with 1 SPAM® Maple Flavored round, a dollop of malt vinegar mousse, and a few reserved fried capers. Drizzle with hot honey and sprinkle with parsley.

SPAM® Classic Mini Korean Corndogs

🕐 **TIME:** 1 HOUR   🍴 **YIELD:** 15 SERVINGS

Take the classic corndog for a flavorful Korean twist that's bound to tantalize your taste buds. Inside each bite-sized delight, you'll discover the irresistible combo of SPAM® Classic and melty mozzarella cheese, perfectly encased in a crispy coat of crushed ramen noodles or panko breadcrumbs. It's a textural masterpiece that'll have you hooked at first crunch.

INGREDIENTS

- 16 food-grade craft sticks
- 1 (12-ounce) can SPAM® Classic cut lengthwise into 4 thick slices, each slice quartered to make 16 pieces
- 8 ounces mozzarella cheese cut into 16 (1-inch x 2-inch) pieces
- 1¼ cups flour
- ¼ cup sugar, divided
- 2 teaspoons baking powder
- ¼ teaspoon salt
- 1 egg
- ¾ cup milk
- Oil for deep frying
- 2 cups panko breadcrumbs
- 2 cups crushed ramen noodles
- Fresh cilantro

SRIRACHA MAYONNAISE

- ½ cup Japanese-style mayonnaise
- 2 tablespoons sriracha sauce
- 1 tablespoon honey

RED CURRY COCONUT SAUCE

- ¼ cup coconut milk
- ¼ cup Japanese-style mayonnaise
- 1 tablespoon red curry paste
- Fresh chopped cilantro, if desired

DIRECTIONS

1. On each of 16 craft sticks, skewer 1 SPAM® Classic piece and 1 cheese piece. Place on tray. Cover and refrigerate.

2. In bowl, whisk together flour, 2 tablespoons sugar, baking powder, and salt. Mix in egg and milk until thick and smooth. Batter should be on the thick side.

3. In large saucepan, heat oil over medium-high heat to 350°F. Place panko breadcrumbs in a shallow dish. Place crushed ramen noodles in another shallow dish.

4. Dip SPAM® Classic sticks into batter, turning until coated. Immediately roll in breadcrumbs or noodles, until very well covered.

5. Working in batches, gently drop battered SPAM® Classic sticks into hot oil. Fry 2 to 3 minutes or until golden brown. Remove to rack and sprinkle liberally with remaining sugar.

6. Make sriracha mayonnaise by combining ingredients in a small bowl. Then, make red curry coconut sauce by combining ingredients in a small bowl. Serve the mini corndogs with the mayonnaise and sauce. Garnish with cilantro.

SPAM® Maple Flavored Baked Brie

 TIME: 40 MINUTES   **YIELD:** 10 SERVINGS

 Serve up an extra dose of yum at your next event with SPAM® Maple Flavored Baked Brie! This soft and gooey dip combines the sweet and savory flavors of apples, pecans, rosemary, and sizzling SPAM® Maple Flavored.

INGREDIENTS

- ½ (12-ounce) can SPAM® Maple Flavored, coarsely chopped
- 2 tablespoons butter
- 1 small tart apple, peeled and sliced
- 3 tablespoons chopped pecans
- 1 teaspoon chopped fresh rosemary
- 1 round (8 ounces) Brie cheese
- Assorted crackers

DIRECTIONS

1. Heat oven to 400°F.
2. In medium skillet over medium-high heat, cook SPAM® Maple Flavored 3 to 5 minutes, or until browned and crisped. Remove from skillet.
3. In same skillet over medium heat, melt butter. Add apple and pecans. Cook, stirring, 5 to 7 minutes or until apple is tender. Stir in rosemary.
4. Cut Brie horizontally in half; place bottom half in a 9-inch pie plate. Top with half of the apple mixture and half of the reserved SPAM® Maple Flavored; replace Brie top. Top with remaining apple mixture and remaining SPAM® Maple Flavored.
5. Bake, uncovered, 8 to 10 minutes or until cheese begins to melt. Serve warm with crackers.

Spicy SPAM® Bites

 TIME: 50 MINUTES **YIELD:** 24 SERVINGS

 Spice up your appetizer game with our flavorful SPAM® Bites. Grated SPAM® Hot and Spicy combines with perfectly cooked Jasmine rice, eggs, Mexican blend and sharp Cheddar cheese, dried chives, and parsley. Coated in a crunchy mix of panko breadcrumbs, finely chopped pecans, and Cajun seasoning, these bites are baked to golden perfection. Serve with a side of ranch and blue cheese salad dressing for a delicious dipping experience.

INGREDIENTS

- 1 package boil-in-bag Jasmine rice
- 1 (12-ounce) can SPAM® Hot and Spicy, grated
- 1 tablespoon dried chives
- 1 cup shredded Mexican blend cheese
- 1 cup shredded sharp Cheddar cheese
- 1 egg plus 2 egg whites
- 1½ cups panko breadcrumbs
- ¾ cup finely chopped pecans
- 2 tablespoons finely chopped parsley
- 2 teaspoons Cajun seasoning
- Ranch and blue cheese salad dressing, for dipping

DIRECTIONS

1. Preheat oven to 375°F.

2. Prepare the rice as the package directs, then drain rice and set aside.

3. Place the grated SPAM® Hot and Spicy and the chives in a large nonstick skillet and cook until the SPAM® mixture is lightly browned; set aside to cool slightly.

4. In a mixing bowl, combine the rice and SPAM® Hot and Spicy mixture, and then add the shredded cheeses and 1 egg, mixing together until mixture is well combined. Shape the SPAM® mixture into small bite-sized balls and place them on a baking sheet lined with parchment paper.

5. In another bowl, beat the egg whites until frothy.

6. In another bowl, combine the breadcrumbs, pecans, parsley, and Cajun seasoning until well blended.

7. Dip each SPAM® ball into the egg whites and coat them with the bread crumb mixture, then return them to the parchment-lined baking pan. Bake at 375°F for 15 minutes or until lightly browned.

8. To serve, place a toothpick in the center of each meatball and serve with ranch and blue cheese salad dressing for dipping.

SPAM® Musubi Crunchy Roll

TIME: 1 HOUR   **YIELD:** 4 SERVINGS

The sweet, tangy, and savory flavors of this crunchy appetizer will take your taste buds on a delectable rollercoaster, leading to a sizzling destination.

INGREDIENTS

- 2 tablespoons soy sauce
- 2 tablespoons sugar
- 1 (12-ounce) can SPAM® Classic, cut into 8 slices
- 3 cups cooked white sushi rice
- 4 sheets nori, cut in half
- 2 eggs, beaten
- 2 cups panko breadcrumbs
- Vegetable oil
- ¾ cup sriracha mayonnaise
- ¾ cup unagi sushi sauce
- 2 teaspoons sesame seeds
- 1 cup shrimp chips, crushed
- ¼ cup chopped green onion

DIRECTIONS

1. In small bowl, combine soy sauce and sugar.

2. In large skillet over medium-high heat, cook SPAM® Classic slices 3 to 5 minutes or until browned. Add soy sauce and sugar mixture, cook 1 to 2 minutes or until slices are glazed. Remove from skillet.

3. Place SPAM® Classic slice and ⅓ cup rice into musubi press, or plastic wrap lined SPAM® can, and press down. Remove from press on top of halved nori sheet. Wrap nori around musubi, moistening edge of nori to adhere together. Repeat to make 8.

4. Place eggs and breadcrumbs in separate shallow dishes. Dip and roll each musubi in egg then in panko.

5. In large skillet over medium-high heat, heat 1 inch vegetable oil. Fry musubi in oil, turning to fry each side, 3 to 5 minutes or until golden brown.

6. Slice each musubi into 4 slices. Line up 8 slices on 4 serving plates. Drizzle each with sriracha mayonnaise, unagi, sesame seeds, shrimp chips, and green onions.

Wonderful SPAM® Wontons

TIME: 1 HOUR, 5 MINUTES   **YIELD:** 8 SERVINGS

Filled with sizzled SPAM® Classic, potatoes, and savory seasonings, these wonderful wontons are a SPAMTASTIC™ treat!

DIRECTIONS

1. Heat oven to 400°F. Place two baking sheets in the oven and heat for 10 minutes.

2. Meanwhile, in a saucepan, combine the first 10 ingredients. Bring the mixture to a boil over medium heat, stirring occasionally.

3. Once boiling, reduce heat and simmer, stirring occasionally, for 8 minutes or until the potato is tender. Take off heat and let cool.

4. Place a colander over a large bowl and place the SPAM® mixture in the colander to drain. Discard the liquid.

5. Finely chop the SPAM® mixture with a knife or pulse twice in a food processor until finely chopped.

6. In a bowl, whisk together the cornstarch and cold water.

7. Working with 1 wonton wrapper at a time, spoon 1 tablespoon of SPAM® mixture into the center of each wrapper (Cover remaining wrappers with damp towel to keep them moist). Moisten the edges of the wrappers with the cornstarch mixture. Bring opposite corners together and pinch the points to seal, forming triangles.

8. Remove the baking sheets from oven and coat with cooking spray. Arrange the filled wonton wrappers in a single layer on baking sheets and coat the wonton wrappers with cooking spray.

9. Bake, turning once, for 8 minutes or until golden brown. Garnish with cilantro.

INGREDIENTS

- 1 (7-ounce) can SPAM® Classic, diced
- 1 cup chicken broth
- 1 clove garlic, minced
- 18 leaves fresh cilantro
- 1 cup onion, finely chopped
- 1 cup red potato, finely chopped
- ¼ teaspoon ground allspice
- ¼ teaspoon ground cumin
- ¼ teaspoon pepper
- ¼ teaspoon salt
- 1 tablespoon cornstarch
- 1 tablespoon cold water
- 36 wonton wrappers
- 1 tablespoon fresh cilantro, finely chopped

LUNCH

76 SPAM® Fried Nice!

77 SPAM® Classic and Beef Ramen

78 The 2-Step SPAM® Grilled Cheese

79 Savory SPAM® Classic with Ramen

80 Pulled SPAM® BBQ Sandwich

81 Teriyaki Katsu SPAM® Musubi

82 SPAM® Western Pasta Salad

83 SPAM® Classic and Gnocchi Soup

84 SPAM® Spuds

85 SPAM® Kimchi Fried Rice Musubi

86 Bow Tie SPAM® Salad

87 SPAM®LT

88 Toasted SPAM® Classic and Cheese Sandwiches

89 SPAM® Mahalo Cups

90 SPAMBURGER™ Sloppy Joes

91 SPAM® PB&J

92 SPAM® Bánh Mi

93 SPAM® Mac 'n' Cheese Musubi

94 Hawaiian SPAM® Sliders

95 SPAM® Grilled Cheese with Brie and Peaches

96 Hot Pressed Cuban SPAM®wich

97 LONO Spring Roll Musubi

98 Pineapple SPAM® Musubi Squares

99 SPAM® Corn Chowder

100 SPAM® Egg Salad Sandwich Spread

101 SPAM® Gyros

102 SPAM® Maple Flavored Grain Bowl

103 SPAM® Panini

104 SPAM® Tamago Sandwich

105 SPAM® Wild Rice Salad

106 Asian SPAM® Slaw with Noodles

107 SPAM® Classic and Kimchi Fried Rice Balls

SPAM® Fried Nice!

🕐 **TIME:** 30 MINUTES   🍴 **YIELD:** 4 SERVINGS

 Feeling fried at the end of a long day? Well, turn the meaning of feeling fried upside-down with irresistible SPAM® Fried Nice. Now feeling fried means you're more than satisfied and your taste buds are delightfully entertained. You'll want to feel fried every day of the week!

INGREDIENTS

- 1 (12-ounce) can SPAM® Teriyaki, diced
- 2 tablespoons vegetable oil, divided
- 2 eggs, beaten
- ¼ cup diced carrots
- ¼ cup chopped green onions
- ¼ cup frozen peas, thawed
- ¼ cup chopped red bell pepper
- 2 cups cooked rice
- 3 tablespoons HOUSE OF TSANG® Soy Sauce

DIRECTIONS

1. In large skillet, heat 1 tablespoon oil. Add eggs. Cook, stirring, to desired doneness. Remove from skillet and set aside.

2. In same skillet, heat remaining 1 tablespoon oil. Cook SPAM® Teriyaki, carrots, green onions, and bell pepper 4 minutes or until vegetables are tender.

3. Stir in rice and egg. Sprinkle with soy sauce. Heat thoroughly.

4. Garnish as desired with additional green onion.

SPAM® Classic and Beef Ramen

 TIME: 20 MINUTES   **YIELD:** 6 SERVINGS

 Pork up your beef ramen in an instant with the delicious flavor of the SPAM® brand. You're going to need more than a spoon to enjoy this hearty soup. It's brimming with slices of sizzled SPAM® Classic, fried eggs, and green onions in a savory broth. The result is satisfaction in a bowl.

INGREDIENTS

- 3 (3-ounce) packages ramen noodle soup, beef flavor
- 1 (12-ounce) can SPAM® Classic, sliced
- 6 fried eggs
- ½ cup sliced green onions

DIRECTIONS

1. Cook noodles according to package directions, including seasoning packet. Divide ramen among 6 individual serving bowls.

2. In a large skillet, over medium-high heat, cook SPAM® Classic 2 to 3 minutes, or until browned.

3. Top ramen and broth with sliced SPAM® Classic, fried egg and green onions.

The 2-Step SPAM® Grilled Cheese

 TIME: 15 MINUTES   **YIELD:** 1 SERVING

 If you can count to 2, you can make this sandwich. If you can't count to 2, here's a quick lesson one, two. Now, all you need is 2 slices of bread, 2 slices of cheese, and 2 slices of SPAM® Classic. Get ready for a grilled cheese that's almost 2 delicious.

INGREDIENTS

- 1 (12-ounce) can SPAM® Classic, sliced into 8 pieces
- 2 slices bread
- 1 tablespoon butter
- 2 slices cheese

DIRECTIONS

1. In a small skillet, cook SPAM® Classic over medium-high heat, turning once, about 5 minutes.
2. Spread one side of each slice bread with butter. Place in skillet, butter-side-down; top 1 slice with cheese. Cook until cheese is melted and bread is toasted. Cover cheese with 2 pieces of SPAM® Classic and 1 slice of cheese. Cover with top slice bread.

Savory SPAM® Classic with Ramen

⏱ **TIME:** 25 MINUTES   🍴 **YIELD:** 4 SERVINGS

Ra-Men! Ra-Women! Lend us your ears! We think ramen is the most ra-mantic dinner. One taste of our Savory SPAM® Classic with Ramen, and you'll be swooning over this recipe. With little heart bubbles and everything.

INGREDIENTS

- 2 (3-ounce) packages ramen noodles Oriental flavor
- 1 tablespoon vegetable oil
- ½ SPAM® Classic, cut into matchstick strips
- 2 tablespoons HOUSE OF TSANG® General Tso Stir-Fry Sauce
- 1 cup snow peas
- 1 cup mushrooms, sautéed
- 1 cup carrots, cut into strips
- 1 egg, hard boiled

DIRECTIONS

1. Cook ramen noodles according to package directions, including seasoning packet.

2. In large skillet over medium-high heat, heat oil. Sauté SPAM® Classic 3 to 5 minutes. Add in General Tso Stir-Fry Sauce during last few minutes to cooking. Remove sizzled SPAM® Classic from the pan.

3. Add snow peas and carrot strips and cook 2 minutes.

4. Add mushrooms, sauté for another 2 minutes.

5. Stir in and reserved noodles & sizzled SPAM® Classic, tossing to coat.

6. Garnish with hard-boiled egg sliced in half.

Pulled SPAM® BBQ Sandwich

 TIME: 15 MINUTES   **YIELD:** 6 SERVINGS

 See the word "pulled" in this recipe's title? It suggests something hard, like pulling a couch up the stairs or pulling a donkey up a hill. Thankfully, this type of "pulled" is a wonderful thing. The kind of barbeque and pork shoulder that's cooked at low heat to be so tender and juicy, you can't be "pulled" away from it.

INGREDIENTS

- ⅓ cup barbecue sauce
- 1 (12-ounce) can SPAM® Hickory Smoke Flavored, finely chopped
- 1 pint coleslaw
- 6 hamburger buns or Kaiser rolls, split and toasted

DIRECTIONS

1. In bowl, mix SPAM® Hickory Smoked Flavored and barbecue sauce.

2. In skillet, heat SPAM® mixture, stirring frequently, until hot.

3. Divide SPAM® mixture evenly among buns; top each with ⅓ cup coleslaw.

Teriyaki Katsu SPAM® Musubi

TIME: 30 MINUTES   **YIELD:** 4 SERVINGS

Not all musubis are alike. This musubi is wrapped in more than just nori, it's sprinkled with Japanese Panko. That texture combined with the flavor of SPAM® Teriyaki make it one of a kind.

INGREDIENTS

- 1 (12-ounce) can SPAM® Teriyaki, cut lengthwise into 8–10 slices
- 3 cups cooked white rice
- 4 sheets nori, cut in half
- 4 cups vegetable oil
- 5 cups panko breadcrumbs
- 4 eggs, beaten
- 1 cup Japanese Mochiko flour
- Siracha mayo, for serving

DIRECTIONS

1. In large skillet over medium-high heat, cook SPAM® slices 3 to 5 minutes or until browned.
2. With moist hands, mold rice into 8 blocks with same dimensions as SPAM® slices. Place SPAM® slices on rice blocks. Wrap each with half sheet of nori, moistening edge of nori to adhere together.
3. In large saucepan, heat oil to 375°F.
4. Place flour, eggs and breadcrumbs in separate shallow dishes. Dip and roll each musubi in flour, then egg and last in panko. Fry in batches 2 to 3 minutes or until golden brown. Serve with siracha mayo.

SPAM® Western Pasta Salad

 TIME: 30 MINUTES   **YIELD:** 8 SERVINGS

 This here Western pasta salad will make your spurs jingle, jangle, jingle. Because it delivers bite after bite of bold savory flavor thanks to SPAM® Classic and its trusty partner, barbecue sauce.

INGREDIENTS

- 1 (12-ounce) can SPAM® Classic, cut into cubes
- 3 cups macaroni, cooked and drained
- 1 cup cubed Cheddar cheese
- 1 cup shredded carrots
- ¾ cup chopped celery
- ¼ cup chopped green bell pepper
- ¼ cup chopped onion
- ½ cup mayonnaise or salad dressing
- 2 tablespoons creamy mustard blend
- 1½ tablespoons barbecue sauce

DIRECTIONS

1. In large bowl, combine macaroni, SPAM® Classic, cheese, carrots, celery, bell pepper and onion; mix well.

2. To make dressing, in small bowl, mix mayonnaise, mustard and barbecue sauce.

3. Toss macaroni mixture with dressing. Cover; refrigerate 1 hour.

SPAM® Classic & Gnocchi Soup

🕐 **TIME:** 40 MINUTES   🍴 **YIELD:** 8 SERVINGS

 Today's soup du jour is SPAM® Classic and gnocchi soup. A bowl full of delightful ingredients like SPAM® Classic, gnocchi, onions, celery, garlic, and carrots are all mixed into a warm chicken broth. It's so good, you'll want it to be the soup du jour every jour!

INGREDIENTS

- 1 (12-ounce) can SPAM® Classic
- 1 tablespoon olive oil
- 1 small onion, diced
- 3 stalks celery, diced
- 3 cloves garlic, minced
- 2 carrots, peeled and shredded
- 4 cups chicken broth
- 1 (16-oz) package potato gnocchi
- 1 (5-ounce) bag baby spinach leaves
- 1 tablespoon cornstarch
- 2 tablespoons cold water
- 2 cups half-and-half cream
- 1 teaspoon salt
- 1 teaspoon pepper

DIRECTIONS

1. In large pot, heat oil; add SPAM® Classic, onion, celery, garlic and carrots. Cook until onion is translucent and SPAM® Classic is browned. Add chicken broth; bring to a simmer.

2. Stir in gnocchi; cook 3 to 4 minutes or until gnocchi begin to float. Stir in spinach until wilted.

3. In small bowl, combine cornstarch and cold water until smooth. Add cornstarch mixture and cream to soup. Cook 5 minutes or until the soup thickens slightly. Season with salt and pepper.

SPAM® Spuds

⏱ **TIME:** 1 HOUR, 15 MINUTES   🍴 **YIELD:** 6 SERVINGS

Your baked spuds will be everyone's buds when they're filled with the inviting combination of cheese, peppers and SPAM® Oven Roasted Turkey.

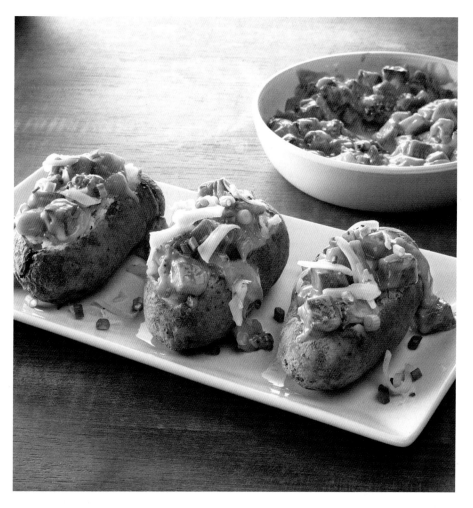

INGREDIENTS

- 6 large baking potatoes
- 1 (12-ounce) can SPAM® Oven Roasted Turkey, diced
- 1 cup frozen broccoli florets, thawed and chopped
- 1 cup frozen carrots, thawed and chopped
- 1 (10.75 ounce) can fiesta nacho cheese soup
- 1 (10.75 ounce) can Cheddar cheese soup
- 1 cup shredded Monterey Jack cheese with peppers
- ½ cup diced green onions

DIRECTIONS

1. Heat oven to 375°F. Pierce potatoes with fork. Wrap potatoes in aluminum foil, place on baking sheet. Bake potatoes 1 hour or until soft.

2. In large skillet over medium heat, cook SPAM® Oven Roasted Turkey 2 to 3 minutes or until lightly browned. Add broccoli, carrots and soup. Cook, stirring frequently, 3 to 5 minutes, or until heated through.

3. Cut tops of potatoes. Fluff insides with fork. Divide SPAM® Oven Roasted Turkey mixture among potatoes. Sprinkle with cheese and green onions.

SPAM® Kimchi Fried Rice Musubi

TIME: 45 MINUTES **YIELD:** 4 SERVINGS

Kimchi and rice are stir fried in a hot pepper paste and topped with slices of SPAM® Classic and cucumber in this deeply delicious musubi masterpiece. Sure, the Mona Lisa is nice, but have you ever seen something as beautiful and savory as this recipe? She's survived thousands of years, but your musubi creation is so tasty it will only last a few minutes.

INGREDIENTS

- 2 tablespoons soy sauce
- 2 tablespoons sugar
- 1 (12-ounce) can SPAM® Classic, cut into 8 slices
- 1 teaspoon vegetable oil
- ½ cup chopped kimchi
- 1 tablespoon gochujang paste
- 3 cups cooked sushi rice
- ¾ cup chopped green onions
- 1 teaspoon sesame oil
- 1 teaspoon sesame seeds
- 1½ cups cucumber slices
- 4 sheets nori, cut in half

DIRECTIONS

1. In small bowl, combine soy sauce and sugar.

2. In large skillet over medium-high heat, cook SPAM® Classic slices 3 to 5 minutes or until browned. Add soy sauce sugar mixture, cook 1 to 2 minutes or until slices are glazed. Remove from skillet and wipe skillet clean.

3. In same large skillet heat oil over medium heat. Add kimchi, and gochujang paste, stir fry 1 to 2 minutes or until combined. Add rice, sesame oil, sesame seeds, and green onions, stir fry, 1 to 2 minutes or until well combined. Remove from heat.

4. Place ⅓ cup rice into musubi press or plastic lined SPAM® Classic can on top of halved nori sheet and press down. Remove press. Place cucumber slices on rice and top with SPAM® Classic slice. Wrap nori around each. Moisten one end slightly to fasten together.

Bow Tie SPAM® Salad

 TIME: 25 MINUTES   **YIELD:** 6 SERVINGS

 All salads have dressing, but not all salads are dressy. This SPAM® salad is so well dressed that it dons multiple bow ties. It is also so well flavored—with chopped bell peppers, honey mustard, and elegant white wine vinegar.

INGREDIENTS

- 1 (12-ounce) can SPAM® Classic, cut into julienne strips
- 2 cups broccoli florets, blanched
- 2 cups cooked bow tie pasta
- ¼ cup chopped bell pepper
- ¼ cup chopped onion
- ¼ cup oil
- ¼ cup white wine vinegar
- 3 tablespoons honey mustard
- 2 tablespoons grated Parmesan cheese
- 1 garlic clove, minced

DIRECTIONS

1. In large skillet, brown SPAM® Classic until lightly browned. In a large non-metal bowl, combine SPAM® Classic, broccoli, pasta, bell pepper, and onion; mix well.

2. In small bowl, with wire whisk or fork, combine remaining ingredients; add to SPAM® mixture and mix well. Cover; refrigerate several hours or overnight.

SPAM®LT

 TIME: 15 MINUTES   **YIELD:** 4 SERVINGS

 Sorry B in BLT, but there's a new sheriff in town. Sheriff SPAM® Classic. And there's only room for one meat in this lettuce and tomato town. So, at high noon, the contest between bacon and SPAM® Classic will be decided. Spoiler alert: SPAM® Classic wins.

DIRECTIONS

1. In large skillet over medium heat, cook SPAM® Classic slices until golden brown on each side.
2. Spread mayonnaise on one side of each toast slice.
3. Layer remaining lettuce leaves, tomato slices and two SPAM® Classic slices over 4 toast slices.
4. Cover with toast, mayonnaise side down.

INGREDIENTS

- 1 (12-ounce) can SPAM® Classic, sliced into 8 pieces
- 8 slices sourdough bread, toasted
- 8 leaves butter lettuce, washed
- ½ cup mayonnaise
- 8 slices tomato
- 1 tablespoon canola oil

Toasted SPAM® Classic and Cheese Sandwiches

 TIME: 15 MINUTES   **YIELD:** 4 SERVINGS

 The grilled cheese sandwich you loved as a kid is all grown up. We layered it with slices of fried SPAM® Classic for a bigger, meatier taste. Next thing you know, you might start feeling like a grown up too and refinance your mortgage. Crazier things have happened. Welcome to the grilled cheese big leagues.

INGREDIENTS

- 1 (12-ounce) can SPAM® Classic, sliced into 8 pieces
- 8 slices cheese
- 8 slices bread, toasted

DIRECTIONS

1. In a large skillet, over medium-high heat, cook SPAM® Classic 3 to 5 minutes, or until browned.
2. Top slices with cheese and cook 1 to 2 minutes or until cheese is melted.
3. Serve on toasted bread.

SPAM® Mahalo Cups

 TIME: 25 MINUTES   **YIELD:** 4 SERVINGS

 Mahalo is Hawaiian for "thank you." And you'll definitely be thanking yourself for making these cups. You'll say to yourself, "Self—thank you for the juicy pineapple; thank you for the crisp vegetables; and thank you for the glorious SPAM® Oven Roasted Turkey!"

INGREDIENTS

- ⅓ cup HOUSE OF TSANG® Hoisin Sauce
- ¼ cup cornstarch
- 4 garlic cloves, minced
- 1 tablespoon fresh grated gingerroot
- 1 (12-ounce) can SPAM® Oven Roasted Turkey, diced
- 1 cup macadamia nuts, finely chopped
- ¼ cup black sesame seeds
- 1 cup red bell pepper, cut into strips
- 1 medium red onion, thinly sliced
- 1 large head green cabbage, separate into 6–8 cabbage leaves (cups) and then shred the remaining cabbage
- 1 cup chopped fresh or canned pineapple

DIRECTIONS

1. In medium bowl, combine hoisin sauce, cornstarch, garlic and ginger. Add SPAM® Oven Roasted Turkey; stir to coat.

2. In shallow dish, combine macadamia nuts and sesame seeds. Toss SPAM® Oven Roasted Turkey in nut mixture.

3. In a large skillet, sauté SPAM® Oven Roasted Turkey in small amount of oil over medium

heat until golden and a little crunchy; set aside.

4. In the same skillet, in a small amount of oil, sauté peppers, onion, and shredded cabbage.

5. Add pineapple; toss to combine. Spoon into cabbage cups; add SPAM® Oven Roasted Turkey. Serve warm or cold.

SPAMBURGER™ Sloppy Joes

TIME: 15 MINUTES **YIELD:** 6 SERVINGS

 Remember those sloppy joes your mom used to make? So messy, but so delicious. It's time to make your own sloppy joes—and your own memories—using spicy SPAM® Lite cut into cubes.

INGREDIENTS

- 1 (12-ounce) can SPAM® Lite, diced
- 1 cup barbecue sauce
- 6 hamburger buns, split and toasted
- 6 (¾-ounce) slices mozzarella cheese
- 1 medium onion, sliced

DIRECTIONS

1. In medium saucepan, cook SPAM® Lite over medium-low heat. Stir in barbecue sauce. Cook, stirring frequently, 5 to 7 minutes or until hot.

2. Spoon SPAM® mixture into buns. Top evenly with cheese and onion.

SPAM® PB&J

TIME: 10 MINUTES   **YIELD:** 1 SERVING

 You'll be surprised—maybe even shocked—at how well SPAM® Less Sodium goes together with peanut butter and jelly. Try it once, and you'll try it a hundred more times.

INGREDIENTS

- 1 (12-ounce) can SPAM® Less Sodium
- White bread
- Smooth peanut butter
- Grape jam
- Butter

DIRECTIONS

1. Slice SPAM® Less Sodium lengthwise into four pieces and fry in skillet until crisp on both sides.

2. Next, toast two slices of bread, then slather on peanut butter and grape jam. Place crisp SPAM® slices between bread.

3. Butter exterior of sandwich and toast in skillet on each of the buttered side. Press down to compress the sandwich. Serve when properly golden brown.

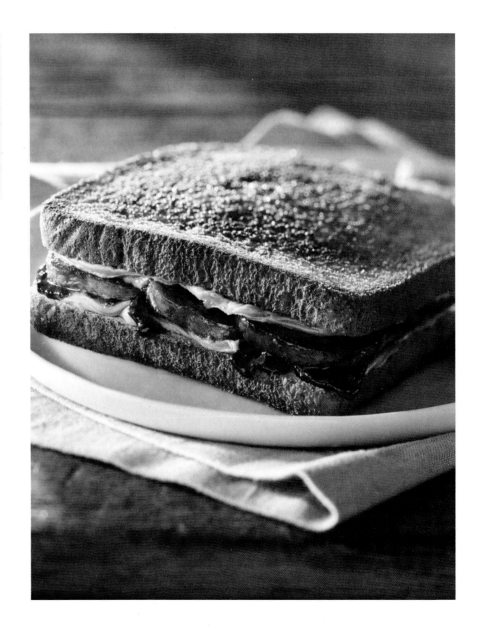

SPAM® Bánh Mi

⏱ **TIME:** 30 MINUTES   🍴 **YIELD:** 4 SERVINGS

If someone wants your SPAM® Bánh Mi sandwich, kindly remind them that it is for "Bánh Me, not Bánh You." Seriously, this is not a sandwich you will want to share. Made with Asian-style steamed buns and sriracha mayo, the flavor will never leave you. Top it off with fried SPAM® Classic, and you'll want to eat it in a safe place where no one can steal it from you.

INGREDIENTS

SMOKED MAYO

- 1 cup canola oil
- 2 egg yolks
- 1 tablespoon fresh lemon juice
- Salt and pepper, to taste

CARROT & CILANTRO SALAD

- ½ pound carrots, grated
- ½ cup cilantro leaves
- 1 jalapeno pepper, sliced or shaved
- 4 tablespoons rice vinegar
- 2 tablespoons sesame seed oil
- Pinch salt
- Pinch black pepper
- Pinch sugar

SANDWICH

- 1 French baguette, cut lengthwise
- 1 (12-ounce) can SPAM® Classic, sliced or shaved
- 1 pound smoked pork, warmed
- ¼ cup ponzu or hoisin sauce

DIRECTIONS

1. Make Smoked Mayo. In bowl, beat together oil and egg yolks. Add lemon juice, salt and pepper to taste. Place in cold smoker (less than 100°) 30 minutes. Stir every 5 to 10 minutes.

2. Make Carrot & Cilantro Salad. In medium bowl, toss grated carrots, cilantro and jalapeño pepper with rice vinegar, sesame seed oil, salt, black pepper and sugar.

3. Assemble sandwich. Spread Smoked Mayo on baguette bottom. Layer SPAM® Classic over mayo. Top with warm smoked pork, ponzu and Carrot & Cilantro Salad. Cover with baguette top. Cut sandwich into 4 portions to serve.

SPAM® Mac 'n' Cheese Musubi

 TIME: 60 MINUTES   **YIELD:** 8 SERVINGS

 The hashtag #MCM used to stand for Man Candy Monday, but there's a new #MCM in town: Mac 'n' Cheese Musubi. We loaded this breaded musubi with macaroni and drizzled it with cheese. That's not just *eye* candy. That's mouth candy.

INGREDIENTS

- 1 (12-ounce) can SPAM® Classic, cut into 8 slices
- 3 cups cooked white sushi rice
- 4 sheets nori, cut in half
- 1½ cups HORMEL® Macaroni and Cheese
- 1 cup flour
- 4 eggs, lightly beaten
- 3 cups panko breadcrumbs
- 4 cups vegetable oil
- 1 cup cheese sauce, warmed
- Cayenne hot sauce

DIRECTIONS

1. In large skillet over medium-high heat, cook SPAM® Classic slices 3 to 5 minutes or until browned.

2. Place ⅓ cup rice into musubi press, or plastic wrap lined SPAM® Classic can and press down. Spoon 2 tablespoons macaroni and cheese on top of rice and top with one slice of SPAM® Classic and press down. Remove from press on top of halved nori sheet. Wrap nori around musubi, moistening edge of nori to adhere together. Repeat to make 8.

3. Place flour, eggs and breadcrumbs in separate shallow dishes. Dip and roll each musubi in flour, then egg and last in panko.

4. In large saucepan heat oil to 375°F. Fry coated musubi 2 at a time, 1 to 2 minutes or until golden brown. Slice each in 2 on the diagonal.

5. Drizzle with cheese sauce and hot sauce.

Hawaiian SPAM® Sliders

TIME: 30 MINUTES   **YIELD:** 12 SERVINGS

Mango meets SPAM® Classic in a match made in Hawaiian heaven.

INGREDIENTS

- 1 (12-ounce) can SPAM® Classic, cut into six slices
- 12 Hawaiian dinner rolls or slider buns, split and toasted
- 1 large mango, peeled and sliced into 12 pieces and cut in half
- 1 ripe avocado, peeled and sliced into 12 pieces and cut in half, or ⅓ cup WHOLLY® Guacamole
- 6 tablespoons Hawaiian-style barbecue sauce

DIRECTIONS

1. In a large skillet over medium heat cook SPAM® Classic 2 to 3 minutes, or until lightly browned. Cut each slice in half.

2. Place one slice of SPAM® Classic on each roll.

3. Top with sliced mango and avocado. Drizzle with barbecue sauce.

SPAM® Grilled Cheese with Brie and Peaches

 TIME: 15 MINUTES   **YIELD:** 4 SERVINGS

 Who knew a humble grilled cheese sandwich could be so refined? Melted Brie and sweet peaches unite to raise this concoction to gourmet heights.

INGREDIENTS

- 8 slices of sourdough bread
- 4 tablespoons butter room temperature
- 8 ounces Brie, sliced
- 2 large peaches, thinly sliced
- 4 tablespoons honey mustard
- 1 (12-ounce) can SPAM® Less Sodium, thinly sliced

DIRECTIONS

1. Prepare grill for medium high heat.
2. Griddle SPAM® Less Sodium to golden brown each side, about three minutes per side. Set aside.
3. Butter one side of each slice of bread. Assemble sandwiches starting with bread butter side out, Brie, cooked SPAM® Less Sodium, smear of honey mustard, topped with bread butter side out.
4. Place sandwiches on the grill. Cook till bread is toasted golden brown and cheese melts, roughly 3 minutes per side.

Hot Pressed Cuban SPAM®wich

 TIME: 20 MINUTES **YIELD:** 1 SERVING

 This Cuban SPAM®wich has all the flavor you'll ever need. Made with kosher dill pickles, Swiss cheese, and a spicy mustard, you'll want to eat these all day.

INGREDIENTS

- 1 (6-inch) soft French roll
- 2 ounces Swiss cheese, thinly sliced
- 3 ounces SPAM® Classic, sliced thin on a meat slicer
- 2 ounces kosher dill pickle, thinly sliced lengthwise
- 2 teaspoons spicy prepared mustard
- 2 tablespoons of softened butter, unsalted

DIRECTIONS

1. Preheat a flattop grill or panini press to 375°F or to medium high.
2. Cut the roll in half and place 1 ounce of cheese on the bottom half, then layer the thinly sliced SPAM® Classic on top, folding it as you go down the bread.
3. Top the SPAM® Classic with the pickle slices and the remaining 1 ounce of cheese.
4. Spread the mustard on the roll, then top the roll and place on sandwich.
5. Brush butter on both sides of the bread, and place on the grill for 2 minutes. While grilling, firmly press down on the sandwich.
6. After one side has turned golden brown and crispy, flip the sandwich and grill for 2 to 3 minutes longer while pressing down.

LONO Spring Roll Musubi

🕐 **TIME:** 30 MINUTES   🍴 **YIELD:** 8 SERVINGS

 Melding the portability of a musubi with the flavors of a spring roll, carrots, daikon, cucumber, vermicelli noodles, and fresh mint leaves set this musubi apart.

INGREDIENTS

- 1 (12-ounce) can SPAM® Less Sodium, cut into 8 slices
- 3 cups cooked sushi rice
- 4 sheets nori, cut in half
- ¾ cup shredded carrots
- ½ cup julienned pickled daikon
- 1 small cucumber, thinly sliced
- 8 ounces vermicelli noodles, cooked and drained
- ½ cup fresh mint leaves
- ½ cup peanut sauce

DIRECTIONS

1. In large skillet, over medium-high heat, cook SPAM® Less Sodium 3 to 5 minutes or until browned. Remove from skillet.

2. Place ⅓ cup rice into musubi press or plastic lined SPAM® can on top of halved nori sheet and press down. Top with carrot, daikon, cucumber, vermicelli, and mint leaves.

3. Spread peanut sauce evenly on one side of SPAM® Less Sodium slice; place sauce side down on top of musubi stack. Remove press.

4. Wrap nori around each. Moisten one end slightly to fasten together. Repeat to make 8.

Pineapple SPAM® Musubi Squares

 TIME: 40 MINUTES   **YIELD:** 9 SERVINGS

 Enjoy island flavor in every bite with these musubi squares! Slices of SPAM® Classic are marinated in soy sauce and pineapple juice before a sear in the frying pan and finished in a bed of rice wrapped in nori.

INGREDIENTS

- 1 (12-ounce) can SPAM® Classic, sliced into 9 slices
- ¼ cup soy sauce
- ½ cup canned crushed pineapple with juice, divided
- 4 sheets nori

MUSUBI RICE

- 2 cups short-grain sushi rice
- 2 cups water
- ½ sheet nori
- ¼ cup unseasoned rice vinegar
- 4 teaspoons sugar
- 1 teaspoon salt

DIRECTIONS

1. Rinse rice in a fine mesh strainer until the water runs clear. Drain.

2. Cook rice and nori according to package directions in a rice cooker or pressure cooker or on the stove. Place cooked rice in large bowl.

3. In small saucepan over medium-high heat, combine vinegar, sugar, and salt until the sugar dissolves. Drizzle vinegar mixture over cooked rice. Gently fold rice to combine. Cover rice with damp paper towel and let cool to room temperature.

4. Cut SPAM® Classic slices in half to equal 18 SPAM® Classic squares.

5. In large shallow dish, combine ¼ cup crushed pineapple with juice and soy sauce. Add SPAM® Classic pieces to dish. Let marinate 10 to 15 minutes.

6. Cut nori into strips to match width of SPAM® Classic pieces.

7. In large skillet over medium-high heat, cook SPAM® Classic pieces, adding marinade and turning frequently, 4 to 6 minutes or until SPAM® Classic pieces are browned and beginning to caramelize. Remove from heat.

8. On work surface, lay 2 nori strips the width of musubi press. Place press over strips.

9. Add ⅓ cup musubi rice to press. Press rice down. Top rice with small spoonful of pineapple soy cooking mixture. Top with 2 SPAM® Classic pieces, side by side. Use press to hold musubi down and pull mold upward to unmold the musubi. Wrap nori around musubi, using a small amount of water to seal ends. Cut through middle of rice to form 2 musubi pieces. Repeat with remaining ingredients to form 18 musubi pieces.

10. Garnish each musubi piece with small amount of remaining crushed pineapple, drained.

SPAM® Corn Chowder

🕐 **TIME:** 45 MINUTES   🍴 **YIELD:** 8 SERVINGS

Experience the comforting warmth of our SPAM® Corn Chowder—a delightful blend of cubed SPAM® Classic, sautéed onions, butter, diced potatoes, chopped green bell pepper, cream-style corn, and milk. This hearty chowder is a satisfying bowl of goodness, perfect for chilly days.

INGREDIENTS

- 1 cup chopped onion
- 1 tablespoon butter or margarine
- 2 cups peeled and diced potatoes
- 1 green bell pepper, chopped
- 2 (15-ounce) cans cream-style corn
- 3 cups milk
- 1 (12-ounce) can SPAM® Classic, cubed

DIRECTIONS

1. In 3-quart saucepan, sauté onion in butter over medium heat for 5 minutes or until golden brown.
2. Add potatoes and green pepper. Cook and stir 2 minutes.
3. Add corn and milk. Bring to a boil.
4. Reduce heat and simmer for 15 minutes or until potatoes are tender, stirring occasionally.
5. Stir in SPAM® Classic. Simmer 2 minutes.

SPAM® Egg Salad Sandwich Spread

 TIME: 1 HOUR, 5 MINUTES   **YIELD:** 2–4 SERVINGS

 This tasty new spin on SPAM® Classic and eggs features mayonnaise, sweet pickle relish, and of course, spectacular SPAM® Classic! We won't have to egg you on to enjoy this delightful SPAM® Egg Salad Sandwich Spread for your next meal.

INGREDIENTS

- 1 (12-ounce) can SPAM® Classic, finely chopped
- 4 hard cooked eggs, finely chopped
- ⅓ cup mayonnaise
- 2 tablespoons celery, finely chopped
- 2 tablespoons sweet pickle relish
- 1 teaspoon prepared mustard
- 1 teaspoon minced onion
- 1 teaspoon sugar
- Pepper to taste
- Bread, crackers, or toasted English muffins

DIRECTIONS

1. In a large bowl, combine the SPAM® Classic and remaining ingredients.
2. Cover and refrigerate at least 1 hour, or up to 24 hours.
3. Spread on your favorite bread, crackers, or toasted English muffins.

SPAM® Gyros

 TIME: 30 MINUTES   **YIELD:** 8 SERVINGS

  Even if you can't pronounce "gyro," you can still make ones with pronounced flavor. Simply sizzle up thin slices of SPAM® Classic and SPAM® Oven Roasted Turkey and toss them on pita rounds, topping things off with a zesty lemon and yogurt mix. It's a Mediterranean taste worthy of a Greek god.

INGREDIENTS

- 1 (12-ounce) can SPAM® Classic, sliced thinly
- 1 (12-ounce) can SPAM® Oven Roasted Turkey, sliced thinly
- 2 cups plain Greek yogurt
- 1 cucumber; peeled, seeded, and shredded
- 2 tablespoons lemon juice
- 1 teaspoon garlic powder
- ½ teaspoon dried dill weed
- ½ teaspoon salt
- ¼ teaspoon pepper
- 8 pita bread rounds
- Suggested toppings; shredded lettuce, chopped tomato, chopped red onion, chopped cucumbers, feta cheese

DIRECTIONS

1. In large skillet over medium-high heat, cook SPAM® Classic and SPAM® Oven Roasted Turkey in batches for 2 to 3 minutes or until lightly browned and crisped. Then set aside.

2. In medium bowl, mix yogurt, cucumber, lemon juice, garlic powder, dill weed, salt, and pepper until combined.

3. Place SPAM® Classic and SPAM® Oven Roasted Turkey on pita rounds. Serve with yogurt mixture. Top with suggested toppings.

SPAM® Maple Flavored Grain Bowl

⏱ **TIME:** 40 MINUTES　　🍴 **YIELD:** 4 SERVINGS

 On days that end in Y, start them with *MMM*. Enjoy cubes of SPAM® Maple Flavored, quinoa, brussels sprouts, apple, cranberry, pecans, and more, topped with a maple-orange vinaigrette.

INGREDIENTS

- 1 (12-ounce) can SPAM® Maple Flavored, cubed
- 2 cups cooked quinoa
- 2 cups quartered, roasted brussels sprouts
- 1 Gala apple, sliced
- 1 cup dried cranberries
- 1 cup chopped pecans, toasted
- 1 small red onion, chopped

MAPLE-ORANGE VINAIGRETTE

- 2 tablespoons maple syrup
- 2 tablespoons orange juice
- 2 tablespoons apple cider vinegar
- 2 teaspoons Dijon mustard
- ½ teaspoon sea salt
- ½ teaspoon ground black pepper
- ⅓ cup olive oil

DIRECTIONS

1. In large skillet, over medium-high heat, cook cubed SPAM® Maple Flavored 3 to 5 minutes or until browned.
2. Divide prepared SPAM® Maple Flavored cubes, quinoa, brussels sprouts, apple, cranberries, pecans, and red onion among 4 individual serving bowls.
3. To make maple-orange vinaigrette, combine ingredients in small jar. Cover and shake to combine. Serve alongside grain bowls.

SPAM® Panini

TIME: 30 MINUTES **YIELD:** 4 SERVINGS

 Any day can be Fryday when you're enjoying the savory deliciousness of SPAM® Classic, tomatoes, bell peppers, and pepperoncini between two slices of crispy Italian bread.

INGREDIENTS

- 1 (12-ounce) can SPAM® Less Sodium, sliced into 8 slices
- 8 slices Italian-style bread
- 2 tablespoons olive oil
- 2 tablespoons Italian dressing
- 2 tablespoons mayonnaise
- 8 slices provolone cheese
- 8 slices tomato
- ½ cup roasted red bell pepper strips
- ½ cup sliced pepperoncini

DIRECTIONS

1. In large skillet over medium-high heat, cook SPAM® Less Sodium slices 3 to 5 minutes or until browned.
2. Heat panini maker or stovetop panini grill according to manufacturer's directions.
3. Brush one side of bread slices with oil. Place bread, oil side down, on work surface.
4. In a small bowl, mix Italian dressing and mayonnaise. Spread on bread slices on work surface.
5. Top each bread slice with one slice cheese. Top one side of each sandwich with 2 slices SPAM® Less Sodium. Top the other side of each sandwich with 2 slices tomato, 2 tablespoons roasted red bell pepper strips, and 2 tablespoons pepperoncini.
6. Put the 4 sandwiches together.
7. Grill sandwiches in panini maker 5 to 7 minutes or until bread is browned and cheese is melted.

SPAM® Tamago Sandwich

TIME: 40 MINUTES   **YIELD:** 1 SERVING

 Sizzled slices of SPAM® Classic are sandwiched between two soft and fluffy slices of milk bread, filled with a buttery egg filling and soft-boiled eggs in this Japanese favorite. *This recipe was developed in partnership with Tastemade.*

INGREDIENTS

- 2 slices SPAM® Classic
- 4 hard-cooked eggs, peeled
- 5 tablespoons mayonnaise
- ¾ teaspoon salt
- ½ teaspoon sugar
- ⅛ teaspoon finely ground black pepper
- 2 slices white bread
- 1 soft-boiled egg, peeled and sliced lengthwise
- 1 tablespoon chopped chives

DIRECTIONS

1. In small skillet over medium-high heat, cook SPAM® Classic slices 3 to 4 minutes or until crispy and browned.

2. Slice hard-cooked eggs in half lengthwise. Remove yolks to medium bowl. Mash yolks with a fork. Add mayonnaise, salt, sugar, and pepper.

3. Finely chop hard-cooked egg whites. Add to mayonnaise mixture. Stir until well combined.

4. Place SPAM® slices horizontally on one slice bread. Top with soft-boiled egg halves face down. Spread hard-cooked egg mixture over top of soft-cooked egg and spread to cover bread slice.

5. Top with remaining bread slice. Trim crusts. Slice sandwich into thirds. Garnish with chives.

SPAM® Wild Rice Salad

TIME: 2 HOURS   **YIELD:** 6 SERVINGS

You will go wild over this salad! Seriously, if you were stuck out in the wild, you could assemble this recipe. It's made with wild rice, carrots, cranberries, onions, pumpkin seeds, honey, and more! Not to mention the wild flavor of SPAM® Classic. Enjoying this fresh salad will take you back to the wild roots of your great, great, great, great nomadic ancestors.

INGREDIENTS

- 6 cups chicken stock or broth
- 1½ cups wild rice
- Juice of 1 lemon
- 1 (12-ounce) can SPAM® Classic or SPAM® Lite, diced
- 1 cup carrots, sliced into matchsticks
- ½ cup dried cranberries
- 4 green onions, finely chopped
- 6 cups romaine lettuce, chopped
- ½ cup pumpkin seeds, toasted (can substitute sunflower seeds or slivered almonds)

VINAIGRETTE DRESSING

- 3 tablespoons apple cider vinegar
- ¼ cup plus 2 tablespoons canola oil
- 2 tablespoons honey
- ½ teaspoon salt
- ¼ teaspoon ground black pepper

DIRECTIONS

1. In a large stockpot, combine the chicken stock or broth and the wild rice. Bring to a boil. Reduce heat, then cover and simmer for about 45 minutes or until the grains are just opened and tender.

2. Drain any excess liquid from the rice and toss with the lemon juice, and then set aside the rice to cool.

3. Sauté the SPAM® product in a large skillet until lightly browned, and then set aside to cool.

4. Meanwhile, prepare the vinaigrette in small bowl, whisking together the cider vinegar, oil, honey, salt, and pepper.

5. Use a large bowl and add the rice, SPAM® product, carrots, cranberries, and green onions.

6. Add the vinaigrette to the rice mixture and toss together, and then refrigerate for 1 hour.

7. Serve the rice mixture over romaine lettuce and top with pumpkin seeds.

Asian SPAM® Slaw with Noodles

 TIME: 30 MINUTES   **YIELD:** 8 SERVINGS

 All your Chinese takeout favorites are combined into one delicious dish. Edamame, ramen noodles, and an Asian honey vinaigrette create a fantastically seasoned soup. If you had a fortune cookie before this meal, it'd read "your taste buds are in for a treat."

INGREDIENTS

- 1 (12-ounce) can SPAM® Less Sodium, diced
- 2 (3-ounce) packages ramen noodles, cooked and cooled (discard seasoning packet or use to season soup)
- 1 (12-ounce) package chopped coleslaw blend
- 1 (8-ounce) package frozen, shelled edamame soybeans
- ½ cup slivered almonds
- ½ cup thinly sliced green onions

ASIAN HONEY VINAIGRETTE

- ⅔ cup SKIPPY® Creamy Peanut Butter
- ⅓ cup honey
- ⅓ cup rice vinegar
- 2 teaspoons soy sauce
- 1 tablespoon sesame oil
- 1 tablespoon water
- Salt and pepper, to taste

DIRECTIONS

1. In a large bowl, combine the ingredients for the Asian honey vinaigrette dressing; mix well, then set aside.
2. In large skillet, cook SPAM® Less Sodium until crisp and lightly browned; set aside.
3. In large bowl, combine the SPAM® Less Sodium, noodles, coleslaw, edamame, almonds, and green onions. Add the dressing and stir until combined.
4. Refrigerate for several hours until ready to serve.

SPAM® Classic and Kimchi Fried Rice Balls

⏱ **TIME:** 1 HOUR, 20 MINUTES   🍴 **YIELD:** 20 RICE BALLS

 These Kimchi Fried Rice Balls are full of sizzle and spice, and they taste so nice! Diced SPAM® Classic, Korean BBQ Gochujang Bulgogi sauce, kimchi, and cheese are rolled up and deep fried for a delicious crunch. *Created in partnership with Omsom sauces.*

INGREDIENTS

- ½ (12-ounce) can SPAM® Classic, diced
- ½ cup kimchi, chopped
- ¼ cup Korean BBQ gochujang bulgogi sauce*
- 2 cups steamed white rice
- ⅔ cup shredded mozzarella cheese
- ½ sheet nori, shredded
- 2 scallions, thinly sliced

Or try the Omsom Spicy Bulgogi starter

- 1 tablespoon sesame oil
- 1 teaspoon toasted sesame seeds
- 20 (½-inch) cubes mozzarella cheese
- 1 cup panko breadcrumbs
- ½ cup all-purpose flour
- 2 eggs, lightly beaten with 1 tablespoon water
- Oil for deep frying

DIRECTIONS

1. In large skillet over medium heat, cook diced SPAM® Classic 3 to 4 minutes or until lightly browned. Remove to large bowl.

2. In same skillet, add kimchi. Cook 1 to 2 minutes. Stir in Korean BBQ gochujang bulgogi sauce and rice. Cook 1 to 2 minutes. Add to bowl. Stir in shredded cheese, nori, scallions, sesame oil, and sesame seeds. Set aside to cool.

3. Roll rice mixture into balls, about 2 tablespoons each, inserting 1 cheese cube in the center of each. Place on parchment-lined baking sheet. Refrigerate 30 minutes.

4. Place breadcrumbs, flour, and egg mixture in separate bowls. Roll rice ball in flour, shaking off excess. Dip rice ball in egg mixture, and then roll rice ball in breadcrumbs. Repeat with remaining rice balls.

5. In 4-quart saucepan over medium-high heat, heat oil to 375°F. Reduce heat to medium and gently place 4 rice balls into oil. Cook 3 to 4 minutes or until golden brown. Remove rice balls with slotted spoon and place on wire rack. Repeat with remaining rice balls.

DINNER

110 SPAM® Classic Budae Jjigae Army Stew

111 Basic SPAM® with Ramen Noodles

112 SPAMBURGER™ Hamburger

113 SPAM® Cordon Bleu Hawaii Kabobs

114 SPAM® Ramen Burger

115 SPAM® Hawaiian Pizza

116 Sun-Dried SPAM® Pasta

117 Easy SPAM® Pho

118 SPAM® Bo

121 Veggie SPAM® Skewers

122 SPAM® Teriyaki, Pineapple and Red Pepper Kabobs

123 SPAM® Cantonese Sweet and Sour

124 Juicy Lucy SPAMBURGER™ Hamburger

125 SPAM® Hawaiian Skillet

126 SPAM® Tacos

127 SPAM® Tater Tot Casserole

128 SPAM® Musubi Burrito

129 SPAM® Cheesy Macaroni Bake

130 SPAM® Classic One-Skillet Mac and Cheese

131 SPAM® Fried Rice

132 Asian SPAM® and Shishito Kabobs

133 Cauliflower Rice SPAM® Musubi Tacos

134 Colorful SPAM® Skillet

135 General Tso SPAM® with Ramen

136 Polynesian Stir Fry

137 SPAM® and Black Beans with Rice

138 SPAM® Chiladas

139 SPAM® Classic Bao Buns

140 SPAM® Classic Fajitas Sheet Pan Dinner

141 SPAM® Classic Potato and Green Bean Sheet Pan Dinner

142 SPAM® Maple Flavored Cowboy Beans

143 SPAM® Maple Flavored Roasted Brussels Sprouts

144 SPAM® Musubi Pizza

145 SPAM® Pizza Casserole

146 SPAM® Kimchi Fried Rice

147 Surf and Turf SPAM® Musubi

**SPAM® Teriyaki,
Pineapple and Red
Pepper Kabobs**

SPAM® Classic Budae Jjigae Army Stew

 TIME: 30 MINUTES **YIELD:** 4 SERVINGS

 This Korean hot pot favorite is the whole kit and canoodle. It's a flavorful medley of ramen noodles, meats, beans, tofu, and veggies simmering in a savory chicken broth. Get jjigae with it.

INGREDIENTS

- 1 (12-ounce) can SPAM® Classic, sliced
- 1 (8-ounce) can pork and beans
- 7 ounces Kielbasa, sliced
- 1 (16-ounce) package firm tofu, sliced
- 1 cup kimchi, diced
- ½ onion, sliced
- 8 ounces mushrooms, sliced
- 1 (4.2-ounce) package Korean ramen noodle, with seasoning packet
- 2 tablespoons Korean chili flakes
- 1 tablespoon Korean chili paste
- 1 tablespoon minced garlic
- 2 tablespoons soy sauce
- ½ teaspoon black pepper
- 4 cups chicken broth
- ¼ cup sliced green onions
- Hot cooked rice

DIRECTIONS

1. In large skillet over medium-high heat, cook SPAM® Classic slices 3 to 5 minutes or until browned.

2. In a large shallow pot or pan, arrange SPAM® Classic slices, pork and beans, Kielbasa, tofu, kimchi, onion and mushrooms. Place ramen noodle on top.

3. In a small bowl, combine ramen seasoning packet, chili flakes, chili paste, garlic, soy sauce and pepper.

4. Add the seasoning mixture to the pot and pour chicken stock over.

5. Bring the pot to a boil over medium-high heat; cook, stirring in the seasoning and noodles for 5 to 6 minutes or until noodles are tender and stew is heated through. Garnish with green onions. Serve with rice.

Basic SPAM® with Ramen Noodles

 TIME: 25 MINUTES   **YIELD:** 6 SERVINGS

 Remember in college when you lived off of ramen noodles? Well, guess what, you're ready to graduate to a more refined dish. These ramen noodles are topped with SPAM® Classic, sautéed broccoli, bell peppers, and sweet chili dipping sauce. Congrats, grad!

INGREDIENTS

- 3 (3-ounce) packages ramen noodles soup, chicken flavor
- 1 (12-ounce) can SPAM® Classic, cubed
- 1 tablespoon olive oil
- 2 cups broccoli florets
- ½ cup yellow bell pepper, diced
- ½ cup cherry tomato halves
- 2 tablespoons HOUSE OF TSANG® Sweet Chili Dipping Sauce

SUGGESTED TOPPINGS

cherry tomato halves, chopped cilantro, sliced jalapeño, soft-cooked eggs

DIRECTIONS

1. Cook noodles according to package directions, including seasoning packet. Drain and discard liquid and set noodles aside.
2. In a large skillet, brown SPAM® Classic 2 to 3 minutes. Remove from skillet. Heat oil over medium heat.
3. Sauté broccoli and bell pepper 3 to 4 minutes or until crisp tender. Stir in tomatoes, sweet chili sauce and reserved noodles, tossing to coat. Stir in SPAM® Classic. Serve with toppings as desired.

SPAMBURGER™ Hamburger

 TIME: 20 MINUTES   **YIELD:** 4 SERVINGS

 Kick ordinary burgers in the buns. This SPAMBURGER™ Hamburger turns your grilling up to 11 and will have you rocking all summer long.

INGREDIENTS

- 1 (12-ounce) can SPAM® Classic
- 4 hamburger buns, split
- 4 slices cheese, if desired

DIRECTIONS

1. Prepare grill.
2. Cut SPAM® Classic into 8 slices.
3. Grill SPAM® slices 5 to 7 minutes or until thoroughly heated, turning once.
4. Place 1 cheese slice on each of 4 SPAM® slices just before removing from the grill. Top with another SPAM® slice. Serve in buns.

SPAM® Cordon Bleu Hawaii Kabobs

 TIME: 55 MINUTES   **YIELD:** 4 SERVINGS

 These Cordon Bleu Hawaii Kabobs will cordon blow your mind. Kabobs with SPAM® Less Sodium cubes, pineapple, and onion are glazed with pineapple preserves and hot pepper flakes. Then they're grilled to perfection with, get this, melted Swiss cheese on top!

INGREDIENTS

- 1 (12-ounce) can SPAM® Less Sodium, cut into 1½-inch cubes
- 2 cups water
- ¼ cup pineapple juice
- 1½ cups rice
- ⅓ cup macadamia nuts, coarsely chopped
- ⅓ cup parsley, chopped
- 1 cup pineapple preserves
- 2 tablespoons white wine vinegar
- 1 teaspoon crushed red peppers
- Salt and freshly ground pepper, to taste
- 1 pineapple, peeled and cored, cut into 1½-inch pieces
- 1 red onion, cut into cut into 1½-inch chunks
- 6 bamboo skewers, soaked in water for 30 minutes
- Olive oil for brushing
- 1 cup shredded Swiss cheese

DIRECTIONS

1. To make rice, in a medium saucepan combine water and juice. Bring to boil. Add rice; stir. Reduce heat to low. Cook, covered 20 minutes; fluff with fork. Add nuts and parsley; stir to combine. Set aside; keep warm.

2. To make pineapple glaze, in a small saucepan heat preserves, vinegar and red peppers, salt, and pepper on medium 3 minutes or until warm, stirring occasionally.

3. Prepare the grill for medium. Thread SPAM® Less Sodium, pineapple, and onion onto skewers. Brush with oil; sprinkle with salt and pepper. Grill 10 to 12 minutes brushing with pineapple glaze and turning occasionally until hot and grill marks appear. Sprinkle hot kebabs with Swiss cheese. Serve with macadamia rice.

SPAM® Ramen Burger

🕐 **TIME:** 25 MINUTES   🍴 **YIELD:** 1 SERVING

Two of the world's greatest foods have finally come together in one recipe: ramen noodles and burgers! The burger is made with ease using a SPAM® Single, then topped with a ramen patty, and flavored with kimchi. Open wide for greatness.

INGREDIENTS

- 1 (3-ounce) package ramen noodles
- 1 large egg, lightly beaten
- 1 tablespoon canola oil
- 1 (3-ounce) package SPAM® Single
- 2 tablespoons kimchi, drained

DIRECTIONS

1. Cook noodles according to package directions, including seasoning packet. Drain and discard liquid. Let noodles stand 15 minutes.

2. Stir in egg and divide mixture in half.

3. Place 2 sheets of plastic wrap in bowls and top with noodles. Fold plastic wrap over noodles and weight with similar bowls. Refrigerate 2 hours. Remove noodles from plastic.

4. In large skillet, heat oil. Cook ramen patties in oil 2 to 3 minutes on each side. Carefully remove to plate.

5. Cook SPAM® slice 2 to 3 minutes or until browned. Top one ramen patty with SPAM® slice and kimchi. Top with remaining ramen patty.

SPAM® Hawaiian Pizza

 TIME: 45 MINUTES   **YIELD:** 8 SERVINGS

 Hawaiian Pizza is enjoyed in Hawaii and across the globe. So what makes this recipe different? We amped up the nod to Hawaii by replacing the ham with even tastier SPAM® Classic. One could say this is the truly Hawaiian, Hawaiian Pizza.

INGREDIENTS

- 1 (10-ounce) can refrigerated all-ready pizza crust
- 1 (6-ounce) package sliced Provolone cheese
- 1 (12-ounce) can SPAM® Classic, cut in thin squares
- 1 (16-ounce) can chunk pineapple, drained
- ½ cup thinly sliced red onion
- ½ cup chopped green pepper

DIRECTIONS

1. Heat oven to 425°F.
2. Grease 14-inch pizza pan or 13 x 9-inch baking pan.
3. Unroll dough; press in prepared pan. Top with cheese.
4. Arrange remaining ingredients over cheese.
5. Bake 25 to 30 minutes or until crust is deep golden brown.

Sun-Dried SPAM® Pasta

⏱ **TIME:** 30 MINUTES 🍴 **YIELD:** 4 SERVINGS

 Based on the title of this recipe, are you worried that it contains sun-dried SPAM® Less Sodium? Chillax. It's the tomatoes that are sun-dried. How else would the tomatoes be dried? By the moon? Let's not over-think this, people. For the best meal under the sun, just make the recipe already!

INGREDIENTS

- Half a 16-ounce box bow-tie pasta, cooked and drained
- 1 (16-ounce) jar sun-dried tomato Alfredo sauce
- 1 (12-ounce) can SPAM® Less Sodium, cut into cubes and browned
- ⅓ pound fresh asparagus spears, cut into 1-inch pieces and lightly cooked
- ½ cup shredded Parmesan cheese

DIRECTIONS

1. In a saucepan, stir together bow-tie pasta, Alfredo sauce, and SPAM® Less Sodium; cook until heated thoroughly. Gently toss in asparagus.

2. Divide SPAM® mixture evenly among 4 plates. Sprinkle with cheese.

Easy SPAM® Pho

⏱ **TIME:** 30 MINUTES   🍴 **YIELD:** 2 SERVINGS

 Pho-cus now! We've got a Pho-ully pho-rmed idea here! It's everything you love about Pho, now with SPAM® Teriyaki! See? We told you! Now don't pho-get!

INGREDIENTS

- ½ (12-ounce can SPAM® Teriyaki, sliced
- 4 ounces uncooked rice noodles
- 3 cups low-sodium chicken broth
- 2 tablespoons HOUSE OF TSANG® Hoisin Sauce
- 2 tablespoons fresh lime juice
- 1 tablespoon fish sauce
- ½ cup thinly sliced white onion
- ½ cup fresh cilantro sprigs
- ½ cup fresh Thai basil sprigs
- ¼ cup sliced green onions
- 1 red chili or red jalapeño, sliced

DIRECTIONS

1. Cook rice noodles according to package directions. Set aside.
2. Cook SPAM® Teriyaki slices according to package directions, until golden.
3. In medium saucepan, over medium heat, add broth and next 3 ingredients. Bring to a boil and remove from heat. Transfer to serving bowls. Divide noodles between serving bowls. Top with SPAM® Teriyaki slices and remaining ingredients.

SPAM® Bo

TIME: 2 HOURS, 45 MINUTES   **YIELD:** 12 SERVINGS

 This dish is full of southern hospitality. It invites you in with the smell of Cajun seasoning. It fills you up with a heaping helping of gumbo. And it gives your taste buds a big warm hug with the flavor of SPAM® Classic!

INGREDIENTS

- 1 (12-ounce) can SPAM® Classic, diced
- ½ pound Andouille sausage, sliced
- 1 teaspoon olive oil
- 1 cup chopped celery
- 1 cup chopped onion
- 1 green bell pepper, chopped
- 2 teaspoons Cajun seasoning, divided
- ½ cup plus 2 tablespoons bacon drippings, divided
- 2 tablespoons butter
- 1 cup flour
- 8 cups beef broth
- 4 cups water
- 2 cloves garlic, minced
- 1 tablespoon sugar

- 1 teaspoon salt
- 2 tablespoons red pepper sauce
- 4 bay leaves
- ½ teaspoon thyme
- 1 (14-ounce) can stewed tomatoes, undrained
- 1 (6-ounce) can tomato sauce
- 2 teaspoons file powder
- 2 (10-ounce) packages frozen cut okra
- 2 tablespoons apple cider vinegar
- 1 (16-ounce) can lump crab meat
- 3 pounds medium raw shrimp, peeled, deveined, tails removed
- 2 tablespoons Worcestershire sauce
- 4 cups cooked rice

SPAM® Bo continued

DIRECTIONS

1. In large skillet over medium-high heat, cook SPAM® Classic and sausage 3 to 5 minutes or until lightly browned. Remove from skillet.

2. In same skillet, add olive oil, celery, onion and bell pepper. Cook over medium heat 5 to 7 minutes or until tender. Stir in 1 teaspoon Cajun seasoning. Set aside.

3. In large skillet over medium heat, melt ½ cup bacon drippings and butter. Add flour, tirring constantly. Cook roux 15 to 20 minutes or until dark brown. Meanwhile, in large soup pot, combine beef broth and water. Bring to a low boil over medium-high heat.

4. Add SPAM® Classic and sausage, onion mixture and garlic to roux. Stir to combine.

Whisk all into the boiling stock mixture. Reduce to a simmer and cook 5 minutes or until starting to thicken.

5. Add sugar, salt, red pepper sauce, bay leaves, thyme, tomatoes with liquid and tomato sauce to soup pot. Simmer 45 minutes, stirring occasionally. Add file powder. Meanwhile, in large skillet over medium-high heat, cook 2 tablespoons bacon drippings, okra, and apple cider vinegar 15 minutes or until tender. Add okra mixture to soup pot. Let mixture simmer, stirring occasionally, 45 minutes. Add crabmeat, shrimp, and Worcestershire sauce. Simmer 5 to 10 minutes. Season with remaining 1 teaspoon Cajun seasoning.

6. Serve with rice.

Veggie SPAM® Skewers

 TIME: 20 MINUTES   **YIELD:** 4 SERVINGS

 Discover the newer way to skewer: replace the meat you usually eat with the festive flavor of SPAM® Jalapeño that's bursting with the lively, zesty taste of green jalapeños.

INGREDIENTS

- 1 (12-ounce) can SPAM® Jalepeno, cut into cubes
- 1 red bell pepper, cut into ¾-inch pieces
- 1 zucchini, cut into ¾-inch pieces
- 1 red onion, cut into ¾-inch pieces
- 2 tablespoons butter
- 2 tablespoons chopped fresh cilantro

DIRECTIONS

1. Prepare grill for medium heat.
2. Thread SPAM® Jalapeño with bell pepper, zucchini, and onion onto 8 to 12 skewers.
3. In small saucepan, melt butter. Remove from heat. Stir in cilantro.
4. Grill skewers, turning occasionally and brushing with butter, 8 minutes or until vegetables are cooked.

SPAM® Teriyaki, Pineapple and Red Pepper Kabobs

 TIME: 30 MINUTES   **YIELD:** 4 SERVINGS

 Grill up kabobs that bring the heat and the sweet. Take meaty chunks of SPAM® Teriyaki and fresh pineapple and skewer them together with zesty red peppers and onions. Then serve them up hot and grill-marked for greatness.

INGREDIENTS

- 1 (12-ounce) can SPAM® Teriyaki, cut into cubes
- 1 red bell pepper cut into ¾-inch pieces
- 1 red onion cut into ¾-inch wedges
- 2 cups fresh pineapple chunks
- ⅓ cup teriyaki sauce

DIRECTIONS

1. Prepare grill for medium heat. Alternately thread SPAM® Teriyaki, bell pepper, onion and pineapple onto 8 to 12 skewers.

2. Grill skewers, turning occasionally and brushing with teriyaki sauce, 8 minutes or until kabobs are hot and well grill marked.

SPAM® Cantonese Sweet and Sour

 TIME: 25 MINUTES   **YIELD:** 4 SERVINGS

 Add a little spicy to your sweet & sour with SPAM® Classic. It's the kind of Asian food that will knock your chopsticks off.

INGREDIENTS

- 2 tablespoons vegetable oil
- 1 carrot, thinly sliced diagonally
- 6 green onions sliced into ¼-inch pieces
- 1 clove garlic, minced
- 3 tablespoons sugar
- 3 tablespoons ketchup
- 3 tablespoons vinegar
- 1 tablespoon cornstarch dissolved in ⅔ cup water
- 1 teaspoon ground ginger
- 1 teaspoon soy sauce
- 1 (12-ounce) can SPAM® Classic, cut into ½-inch cubes
- 1 (8-ounce) can bamboo shoots, drained
- 1 cucumber, cut into ½-inch chunks
- Hot rice, for serving

DIRECTIONS

1. In wok or large skillet, heat oil over medium heat. Add carrot, onions and garlic; cook, stirring occasionally, 4 to 5 minutes or until crisply-tender.

2. Add next 7 ingredients to skillet. Cook, stirring constantly, 5 to 6 minutes or until sauce is thickened. Add SPAM® Classic, bamboo shoots and cucumber. Cook until heated thoroughly. Serve over hot rice.

Juicy Lucy
SPAMBURGER™ Hamburger

 TIME: 10 MINUTES   **YIELD:** 1 SERVING

 Think of the juiciest, most tasty looking burger you can think of. Now think about that same burger, but with glorious SPAM® Classic covered in layers of melted Cheddar cheese. If your mouth isn't watering, you may need to see a mouth doctor.

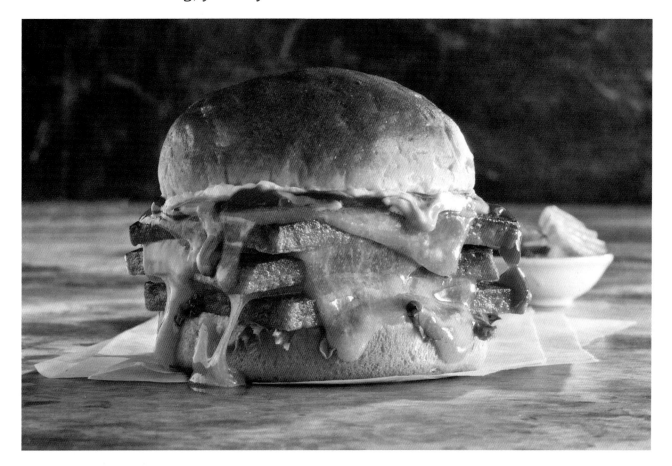

INGREDIENTS

- 3 slices SPAM® Classic
- 1 potato slider bun, split and toasted
- 3 slices Cheddar cheese slices
- Suggested toppings: mayonnaise, mustard, ketchup, lettuce, and pickles

DIRECTIONS

1. Cook SPAM® Classic according to package directions, until golden.
2. Top each SPAM® slice with cheese slice. Stack together.
3. Serve in bun with suggested toppings.

SPAM® Hawaiian Skillet

 TIME: 20 MINUTES   **YIELD:** 4 SERVINGS

 Enjoy the fruits of barely having to labor with this easy SPAM® Hawaiian Skillet. Chopped pineapple, mango and SPAM® with Real HORMEL® Bacon combines sweet and smoky notes in a balsamic glaze. You won't get waves of flavor this big except off Oahu's North Shore.

INGREDIENTS

- 1 (12-ounce) can SPAM® with Real HORMEL® Bacon, diced
- 1 cup chopped pineapple
- 1 cup chopped mango
- ½ teaspoon cumin
- ½ teaspoon smoked paprika
- ½ teaspoon salt
- ½ teaspoon garlic salt
- Hot cooked rice
- Balsamic glaze

DIRECTIONS

1. In large skillet over medium-high heat, cook SPAM® with Real HORMEL® Bacon, pineapple, mango, cumin, smoked paprika, salt and garlic powder 6 to 8 minutes or until nicely browned.

2. Serve over rice. Drizzle with balsamic glaze.

SPAM® Tacos

 TIME: 20 MINUTES   **YIELD:** 5 SERVINGS

 These bold little street tacos go big on pork flavor. Plus they're quick and easy to make with just a few simple ingredients, so don't be surprised if they turn you into a homebody. Who said a street taco can't be a couch taco?

INGREDIENTS

- 1 (12-ounce) can SPAM® Classic, sliced into strips
- 1 small onion, diced
- ½ cup chopped cilantro
- 1 (10-count) package taco size corn tortillas, warmed
- Salsa for serving

DIRECTIONS

1. In large skillet, over medium-high heat, cook SPAM® Classic 3 to 5 minutes or until lightly browned.

2. Place SPAM® Classic in tortillas with onion and cilantro. Serve with salsa.

SPAM® Tater Tot Casserole

 TIME: 1 HOUR, 20 MINUTES   **YIELD:** 8 SERVINGS

 Here's the perfect casserole! It's easy, filling, satisfying, and oozy with cheese and crisp tater tots.

INGREDIENTS

- 1 tablespoon butter
- 1 small yellow onion, diced
- 1 can SPAM® with Real HORMEL® Bacon, cubed
- 12 eggs, beaten
- 3 cups shredded sharp Cheddar cheese
- 1 teaspoon smoked paprika
- 1 teaspoon onion powder
- 1 teaspoon salt
- Black pepper, to taste
- 1 (24-ounce) package frozen tater tots

DIRECTIONS

1. Heat oven to 350°F. Lightly grease a 3-quart baking dish. In medium skillet, over medium-high heat melt butter. Add onions. Cook 3 to 5 minutes or until softened. Remove from pan.

2. In same skillet, cook SPAM® with Real HORMEL® Bacon 3 to 4 minutes, or until crisped and browned. In large bowl combine eggs, cheese, paprika, onion powder, salt and pepper. Whisk until combined. Add onions, SPAM® with Real HORMEL® Bacon, and tater tots tossing to combine.

3. Pour mixture into prepared baking dish. Bake 45 minutes. Broil an additional 10 to 15 minutes or until golden brown on top.

SPAM® Musubi Burrito

⏱ **TIME:** 45 MINUTES   🍴 **YIELD:** 8 SERVINGS

As Hawaii's most popular food, SPAM® Musubi is not only on a roll, now it's in one. Make the burrito version using steamy sushi rice, furikake garnish, and scrambled egg drizzled in sweet unagi sauce. All rolled up burrito-style in crunchy nori for a fistful of fantastic flavor.

INGREDIENTS

- ¼ cup flour
- 2 eggs, beaten
- 1 cup panko breadcrumbs
- 1 (12-ounce) can SPAM® Classic, sliced into strips
- Vegetable oil
- 8 sheets nori
- 3 cups cooked sushi rice
- Furikake
- 4 eggs, scrambled
- 1 cup coleslaw mix
- 1 small cucumber, julienned
- ½ cup French fried onions
- Unagi sauce

DIRECTIONS

1. Place flour, eggs, and breadcrumbs in separate shallow dishes. Dredge SPAM® Classic strips in flour, dip in eggs and roll in breadcrumbs.

2. In a large skillet, pour enough vegetable oil to cover bottom by 1 inch. Heat oil over medium-high heat. Add breaded SPAM® Classic strips to skillet and fry 3 to 5 minutes, turning once, until golden brown. Remove from skillet.

3. Place 1 sheet nori on work surface. With moist hands, spread rice evenly over nori, leaving a ¾ inch strip uncovered on one end. Sprinkle rice with Fuikake.

4. Layer fried SPAM® Classic strips, eggs, coleslaw mix, cucumber, and French-fried onions; drizzle with Unagi sauce; roll up. Repeat with remaining ingredients.

SPAM® Cheesy Macaroni Bake

TIME: 40 MINUTES   **YIELD:** 6 SERVINGS

The best things really do come in threes. There's The Three Musketeers. Three-ring circuses. And rock-paper-scissors. The best-tasting things come in threes as well: macaroni, cheese, and SPAM® Classic. You know what else is amazing? This yummy recipe serves 6—which is 2 times 3!

INGREDIENTS

- 1 (12-ounce) can SPAM® Classic, diced
- 1 tablespoon all-purpose flour
- 2 tablespoons butter or margarine, divided
- ¼ teaspoon dry mustard
- 8 ounces elbow macaroni
- ½ cup fresh breadcrumbs (1 slice)
- 1 pinch ground red pepper (cayenne)
- 2 cups milk
- ⅛ teaspoon paprika
- ½ pound processed sharp American cheese, diced
- ¼ teaspoon salt

DIRECTIONS

1. Heat oven to 400°F. Lightly grease a 2-quart casserole.

2. Cook macaroni according to package directions; drain.

3. In the casserole, stir together SPAM® Classic and macaroni.

4. In a medium saucepan, melt 1 tablespoon butter. Blend in flour, salt, mustard, black pepper, and cayenne until smooth. Stir in milk; cook over medium heat, stirring, until mixture thickens and boils. Add cheese; cook, stirring, until cheese is melted. Pour over SPAM® mixture; mix well.

5. In a microwave-safe bowl, melt remaining 1 tablespoon butter; stir in breadcrumbs and paprika. Sprinkle over macaroni. Bake 20 to 25 minutes.

SPAM® Classic One-Skillet Mac and Cheese

⏰ **TIME:** 30 MINUTES   🍽 **YIELD:** 6 SERVINGS

It's time you upgraded to the latest version of Mac and Cheese. Hearty chunks of fried SPAM® Classic are tossed with creamy, cheesy macaroni and topped with toasted breadcrumbs. This easy one-skillet meal is Mac 2.0.

INGREDIENTS

- 1 (12-ounce) can SPAM® Classic, diced
- 4 cups whole milk
- 2½ cups uncooked elbow macaroni
- 2 cups shredded mild Cheddar cheese
- ½ cup shredded part-skim mozzarella cheese
- 2 ounces cream cheese
- 4 tablespoons butter, divided
- 1 teaspoon Dijon mustard
- ¼ teaspoon cayenne pepper
- Pinch of nutmeg
- 1 teaspoon salt
- 1 cup panko bread crumbs
- 1 tablespoon chopped parsley, if desired

DIRECTIONS

1. Heat broiler to high.
2. In a large broiler-safe skillet, over medium-high heat, cook SPAM® Classic 2 to 3 minutes or until lightly browned. Remove from skillet.
3. In the same skillet, over medium heat, combine milk and macaroni. Bring to a simmer. Cook 5 to 6 minutes, stirring to prevent sticking, until macaroni is tender and mixture has thickened. Remove from heat. Stir in cheeses, 2 tablespoons butter, mustard, cayenne, nutmeg and salt.
4. In a small microwavable bowl, melt remaining 2 tablespoons butter. Add breadcrumbs, stirring to coat. Sprinkle mixture on top of macaroni and cheese.
5. Broil 3 to 5 minutes or until breadcrumbs are golden brown.

SPAM® Fried Rice

TIME: 30 MINUTES   **YIELD:** 8 SERVINGS

You know, just about anything tastes great fried. Eggs. Potatoes. Even bananas. Well, now you can add rice to the list, especially since it's combined with frying-pantastic SPAM® Classic.

INGREDIENTS

- 2 tablespoons canola oil
- 1 small onion, finely chopped
- 2 cloves garlic, minced
- 1 (12-ounce) can SPAM® Classic, cut into cubes
- 2 cups green beans, cut into ¼-inch pieces
- 4 cups chilled cooked rice
- 3 eggs, scrambled
- ¼ cup soy sauce
- 1 pinch salt

DIRECTIONS

1. In wok or deep frying pan, heat oil over high heat. Add onion; cook 3 to 4 minutes or until translucent. Add garlic; stir-fry 30 seconds longer. Add SPAM® Classic; cook 3 minutes longer.

2. Add beans to wok; stir-fry 3 to 4 minutes or until tender. Add rice; cook, stirring, 3 to 4 minutes longer or until heated thoroughly. Add eggs, soy sauce and salt; mix well. Serve immediately.

Asian SPAM® and Shishito Kabobs

 TIME: 30 MINUTES   **YIELD:** 6 SERVINGS

Add a little sizzle to your grill with these Asian SPAM® and Shishito Kabobs. Loaded up with cubes of SPAM® Classic, shishito peppers, and red onion and glazed in a sweet and savory mix of soy sauce, honey, and garlic—these kabobs are a colorful treat for the eyes and the taste buds.

INGREDIENTS

- 3 tablespoons soy sauce
- 3 tablespoons honey
- 1 tablespoon oil
- 2 cloves garlic, minced
- 2 teaspoons grated ginger
- 1 teaspoon sesame oil
- ½ teaspoon crushed red pepper
- 1 (12-ounce) can SPAM® Classic, cubed
- 16 shishito peppers, trimmed and cut in half if necessary
- 1 large red onion, cut into chunks
- Sesame seeds and sliced green onions, for serving
- Hot cooked rice, if desired

DIRECTIONS

1. In small bowl, combine soy sauce, honey, oil, garlic, ginger, sesame oil, and crushed red pepper; mix well.
2. Heat grill to medium heat.
3. Alternately thread SPAM® Classic, peppers, and onion onto 6 skewers.
4. Grill the skewers, turning occasionally and brushing with soy sauce mixture, 8 minutes or until kabobs are hot and well grill marked.
5. Sprinkle with sesame seeds and green onions.
6. Serve with rice, if desired.

Cauliflower Rice SPAM® Musubi Tacos

 TIME: 40 MINUTES　　 **YIELD:** 4 SERVINGS

Musubi tacos? Shell yes! This innovative recipe folds fried nori into a taco shape as it cools then tops it with diced SPAM® Classic. The fusion of flavors will also curl your lips into a taco shape as you smile with delight.

INGREDIENTS

- 1 egg
- 1 cup flour
- 1 cup cold water
- 3 cups vegetable oil
- 8 sheets nori, trimmed with scissors into circular shape
- 1 (12-ounce) can SPAM® Classic, cut in large dice
- 1 teaspoon sesame seeds
- 3 cups cauliflower
- ½ cup water
- 2 tablespoons rice vinegar
- ¾ cup julienned cucumbers
- ¾ cup grated carrots
- Wasabi
- Soy sauce
- Pickled ginger

DIRECTIONS

1. In a medium bowl, whisk the egg. Add the flour and cold water, whisking just enough to blend.

2. In a large saucepan, heat oil to 375°F.

3. Dip one side of a nori sheet in the batter mixture.

4. Carefully fry the nori sheet in hot oil, batter side first, for 1 to 2 minutes, then flip to fry the other side until crisp and curled. Remove the nori from the oil to a paper-towel-lined sheet pan, forming it into a taco shell as it cools. Repeat to make 8 taco shells.

5. In a large skillet, cook the diced SPAM® Classic over medium-high heat for 3 to 5 minutes, or until browned. Sprinkle with sesame seeds.

6. In another large skillet, steam the cauliflower in water over medium heat for 4 to 6 minutes, or until softened. Season with rice vinegar.

7. Divide the cauliflower rice and SPAM® Classic between the nori shells. Top the tacos with cucumber and carrots. Serve with wasabi, soy sauce, and pickled ginger.

Colorful SPAM® Skillet

 TIME: 50 MINUTES **YIELD:** 6 SERVINGS

 Make a dinner that's full of color and flavor. Here's a hearty, satisfying dish that simmers with savory flavor because it's made with SPAM® Less Sodium.

INGREDIENTS

- 1 (10¾-ounce) can cream of celery soup
- 1½ cups water
- 1 tablespoon butter or margarine
- 1 (12-ounce) can SPAM® Less Sodium, cut into cubes
- ¾ cup long-grain rice
- 1 (10-ounce) package frozen peas
- 1 (4.5-ounce) jar sliced mushrooms, drained
- 1 cup shredded Cheddar cheese

DIRECTIONS

1. In a large skillet, combine the soup, water, and butter. Bring mixture to a boil.
2. Add the SPAM® Less Sodium and rice. Reduce heat, cover, and simmer for 18 minutes.
3. Stir peas and mushrooms into skillet, then cover and simmer for 15 minutes or until the rice is cooked through and the peas are heated thoroughly.
4. Sprinkle cheese over the rice mixture and cover. Let stand for 5 minutes or until cheese is melted.

General Tso SPAM® with Ramen

 TIME: 15 MINUTES   **YIELD:** 4 SERVINGS

 Transform your dinner routine with our General Tso SPAM® Classic and Ramen dish. SPAM® Classic is cut into matchsticks and combined with Oriental-flavor ramen noodles, sautéed with vegetable oil, snow peas, and strips of red bell pepper. Elevate the flavors with a drizzle of HOUSE OF TSANG® General Tso Stir-Fry Sauce for a quick and delicious Asian-inspired meal.

INGREDIENTS

- 2 (3-ounce) packages ramen noodles, Oriental flavor
- 1 tablespoon vegetable oil
- ½ (12-ounce) can SPAM® Classic, cut into matchsticks
- 1 cup snow peas
- 1 cup red bell pepper, cut into strips
- 2 tablespoons HOUSE OF TSANG® General Tso Stir-Fry Sauce

DIRECTIONS

1. Cook ramen noodles according to package, including seasoning packet. Drain and discard liquid and set noodles aside.

2. Heat oil in large skillet over medium-high heat and sauté SPAM® Classic for 2 to 3 minutes.

3. Add snow peas and red bell pepper and cook 2 minutes.

4. Stir in General Tso Stir-Fry Sauce and reserved noodles, tossing to coat.

Polynesian Stir Fry

⏱ **TIME:** 20 MINUTES   🍽 **YIELD:** 4 SERVINGS

Indulge in a tropical symphony of flavors with our Polynesian Stir-Fry. SPAM® Lite sizzles alongside succulent pineapple tidbits, a zesty sweet-and-sour sauce, and crisp vegetables. Enjoy this delicious island-inspired delight over a bed of hot, fluffy rice.

INGREDIENTS

- 1 (8-ounce) can pineapple tidbits
- 1 (1.75-ounce) package sweet-and-sour sauce mix
- 1 large onion, sliced
- 1 large green bell pepper, cut into 1-inch strips
- 1 tablespoon vegetable oil
- 1 (12-ounce) can SPAM® Lite
- 1 (8-ounce) can sliced water chestnuts, drained
- 4 cups hot, cooked rice

DIRECTIONS

1. Drain the pineapple, saving the juice. Add water to the juice to make 1 cup. Stir in sweet-and-sour sauce mix.
2. In large skillet, sauté onion and bell pepper in oil over medium heat, stirring constantly, for 4 minutes.
3. Add SPAM® Lite and water chestnuts, then cook for 1 minute longer.
4. Add sweet-and-sour sauce and pineapple, then bring to a boil. Boil for 1 minute.
5. Serve stir-fry over hot rice.

SPAM® and Black Beans with Rice

⏱ **TIME:** 25 MINUTES   🍽 **YIELD:** 6 SERVINGS

 With just three easy steps, you'll have a hot flavorful meal ready in less than 30 minutes, featuring sizzling cubes of SPAM® Classic, black beans, and rice with cumin, cayenne, and Cajun tomatoes.

INGREDIENTS

- 1 cup long-grain rice
- 1 (12-ounce) can SPAM® Classic, cut into cubes
- ½ cup chopped onion
- ½ cup chopped green bell pepper
- 1 tablespoon butter or margarine
- 1 (15-ounce) can black beans, drained and rinsed
- 1 (15-ounce) can Cajun stewed tomatoes
- ½ teaspoon ground cumin
- ⅛ teaspoon ground red pepper (cayenne)

DIRECTIONS

1. Cook rice according to package.
2. Meanwhile, in a large skillet, sauté the SPAM® Classic, onion, and bell pepper in butter until the onion is softened and the SPAM® Classic is lightly browned.
3. Stir in the beans, tomatoes, cumin, and cayenne into skillet. Cook, stirring occasionally, until the beans are heated thoroughly. Serve over hot rice.

SPAM® Chiladas

⏱ **TIME:** 1 HOUR, 10 MINUTES   🍴 **YIELD:** 8 SERVINGS

Spice up your dinner routine with mouthwatering SPAM® Chiladas, featuring grated SPAM® Jalapeño for an extra kick. Sautéed with garlic, green bell pepper, and onions and mixed with black beans, cilantro, and cooked white rice, this flavorful filling is wrapped in tortillas and smothered in LA VICTORIA® Red Enchilada Sauce. Top with a generous helping of Mexican blend cheese, bake until golden, and serve with a side of WHOLLY® Guacamole for a deliciously zesty twist on classic enchiladas.

INGREDIENTS

- 1 (12-ounce) can SPAM® Jalapeño, grated
- 2 tablespoons olive oil
- 1 large onion, finely chopped
- 4 cloves garlic, minced
- 1 green bell pepper, diced
- 1 (15-ounce) can black beans, drained and rinsed
- 2 cups cooked white rice

- 2 tablespoons fresh cilantro, chopped
- 2 cups shredded Mexican blend cheese, divided
- 1 (28-ounce) can LA VICTORIA® Red Enchilada Sauce
- 8 (8-inch) corn or flour tortillas
- WHOLLY® Guacamole to serve

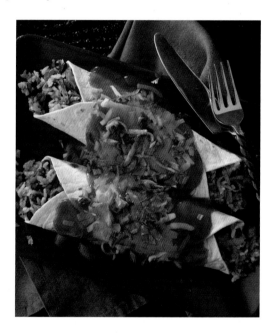

DIRECTIONS

1. Heat oven to 350°F.
2. Set aside about ¼ cup of the grated SPAM® Jalapeño for garnish.
3. In a large skillet, heat oil on medium high. Cook the onion, garlic, and pepper for 5 minutes or until the onion is softened.
4. Add all the grated SPAM® Jalapeño, except for the garnish, and fry for 5 minutes or until browned. Add the black beans, rice, cilantro, and 1 cup of the cheese, stirring until well combined.
5. Spoon ¼ of the enchilada sauce over the bottom of a 9x13-inch baking dish.

6. Heat tortillas and coat with the enchilada sauce.
7. Spoon the SPAM® mixture onto each tortilla, then roll up to enclose the filling. Place each enchilada in the baking dish and pour the remaining enchilada sauce over the tortillas.
8. Top with the remaining shredded cheese. Cover with foil and bake for 40 to 45 minutes or until warmed through.
9. Serve with guacamole, if desired. Sprinkle reserved grated SPAM® Jalapeño over enchiladas.

SPAM® Classic Bao Buns

  TIME: 30 MINUTES   **YIELD:** 8 SERVINGS

 These sizzling sandwiches feature chopped kimchi, creamy mayonnaise, and strips of SPAM® Classic that will have your taste buds asking for seconds. The symphony of flavors builds with freshly peeled carrot and cucumber strips, a drizzle of rice vinegar and sesame oil for that extra zing, and a sprinkle of cilantro and sesame seeds.

INGREDIENTS

- ½ cup kimchi, finely chopped
- ½ cup mayonnaise
- 3 carrots, peeled into strips
- 1 English cucumber, peeled into strips
- 1 teaspoon rice vinegar
- ½ teaspoon sesame oil
- ½ teaspoon salt
- 2 tablespoons chopped fresh cilantro
- Sesame seeds, as desired
- 1 (12-ounce) can SPAM® Classic, sliced into strips
- 8 frozen bao buns, thawed
- ½ cup chopped PLANTERS® Cocktail Peanuts

DIRECTIONS

1. In small bowl, combine kimchi and mayonnaise. Set aside.

2. In large bowl, mix carrots, cucumbers, rice vinegar, sesame oil, salt, cilantro, and sesame seeds.

3. In large skillet over medium-high heat, cook SPAM® Classic 3 to 4 minutes or until browned and crispy.

4. Serve bao buns filled with SPAM® Classic, carrot and cucumber mixture, and kimchi mixture. Sprinkle with peanuts.

SPAM® Classic Fajitas Sheet Pan Dinner

TIME: 40 MINUTES   **YIELD:** 4 SERVINGS

Take your taste buds on a flavor adventure with sizzled strips of SPAM® Classic, cotija cheese, bell peppers, and onions!

INGREDIENTS

- 1 large white onion, cut into strips
- 1 green bell pepper, cut into strips
- 1 red bell pepper, cut into strips
- 3 teaspoons olive oil, divided
- 2 tablespoons taco seasoning mix from a (1.25-ounce) packet, divided
- 1 (12-ounce) can SPAM® Classic, cut into strips
- ¼ cup crumbled cotija cheese
- Chopped cilantro
- Lime wedges
- Fajita-size flour tortillas

DIRECTIONS

1. Heat oven to 425°F. Arrange onion and peppers in a single layer on a large, rimmed baking sheet. Drizzle with 2 teaspoons oil. Sprinkle with 1 tablespoon taco seasoning. Roast vegetables 10 minutes.

2. Drizzle with remaining 1 teaspoon oil and remaining 1 tablespoon taco seasoning. Add SPAM® Classic slices to pan. Roast 8 to 16 minutes or until vegetables are tender and SPAM® Classic strips are lightly browned.

3. Sprinkle with cheese and cilantro. Serve with lime wedges and tortillas.

SPAM® Classic Potato and Green Bean Sheet Pan Dinner

 TIME: 40 MINUTES   **YIELD:** 4 SERVINGS

 Dinner will get two yums up when you can enjoy sizzled slices of SPAM® Classic, chopped Yukon gold potatoes, and green beans in under an hour.

INGREDIENTS

- 1½ pounds small Yukon gold potatoes, chopped
- 2 tablespoons olive oil, divided
- 1 teaspoon salt, divided
- ½ teaspoon pepper, divided
- ½ pound green beans, trimmed
- 1 (12-ounce) can SPAM® Classic, sliced
- ½ cup mayonnaise
- 2 tablespoons grainy Dijon mustard
- 1 tablespoon cider vinegar
- 1 teaspoon maple syrup
- 2 tablespoons chopped parsley

DIRECTIONS

1. Heat oven to 425°F. On a large, rimmed baking sheet, toss together potatoes, 1 tablespoon oil, ½ teaspoon salt, and ¼ teaspoon pepper. Spread out to cover.

2. Bake 30 minutes or until potatoes are tender-crisp. Move potatoes to one side of baking sheet.

3. Add green beans to baking sheet. Drizzle with remaining oil. Sprinkle with remaining salt and pepper. Add SPAM® Classic slices to baking sheet.

4. Bake 15 to 20 minutes, turning SPAM® Classic slices once during baking, or until vegetables are tender and SPAM® Classic slices are golden brown.

5. In small bowl, whisk together mayonnaise, mustard, vinegar, and maple syrup. Stir in parsley. Serve with sheet pan dinner.

SPAM® Maple Flavored Cowboy Beans

⏰ **TIME:** 5 HOURS   🍽 **YIELD:** 10 SERVINGS

These SPAM® Maple Flavored Cowboy Beans are the perfect addition to any BBQ or outdoor gathering! These sweet and savory beans are made with a base of hearty pinto, butter, and kidney beans and are flavored with a mixture of brown sugar, apple cider vinegar, yellow mustard, ketchup, and diced SPAM® Maple Flavored. They're easy to make in a slow-cooker and are sure to be a crowd-pleaser.

INGREDIENTS

- 1 (12-ounce) can SPAM® Maple Flavored, diced
- 1 onion, chopped
- 1 red bell pepper, chopped
- 1 (15-ounce) can butter beans, drained
- 1 (15-ounce) can kidney beans, rinsed and drained
- 2 (15-ounce) cans pork and beans
- 1 (15-ounce) can pinto beans, rinsed and drained
- ½ cup packed brown sugar
- ¼ cup ketchup
- 3 tablespoons apple cider vinegar
- 2 tablespoons yellow mustard
- ½ teaspoon salt
- ½ teaspoon pepper
- Chopped green onions, if desired

DIRECTIONS

1. In large skillet over medium heat, cook SPAM® Maple Flavored 3 to 5 minutes or until crisped and browned. Remove from pan to a 4-quart slow cooker.

2. In same large skillet, over medium-high heat, cook onion and red bell pepper 3 to 5 minutes, or until softened. Add to slow cooker.

3. Add remaining ingredients to slow cooker, except for green onions. Cover and cook on low 4 to 5 hours or until heated through.

4. Serve garnished with green onions, if desired.

5. Alternatively, bake mixture in a casserole dish at 350°F for 40 to 45 minutes or until bubbly.

SPAM® Maple Flavored Roasted Brussels Sprouts

 TIME: 45 MINUTES   **YIELD:** 4–8 SERVINGS

 Served in a balsamic glaze, this veggie-forward dish features brussels sprouts, shallots, garlic, and more with a touch of sweet SPAM® Maple Flavored.

INGREDIENTS

- 1 (12-ounce) can SPAM® Maple Flavored, diced
- 2 tablespoons olive oil
- 1½ pounds fresh brussels sprouts, trimmed and halved
- 4 shallots, quartered
- 4 garlic cloves, crushed
- 1 teaspoon kosher salt
- ½ teaspoon freshly ground pepper
- Balsamic glaze, as desired

DIRECTIONS

1. Heat oven to 425°F.
2. In large bowl, toss together diced SPAM® Maple Flavored and remaining ingredients, except for balsamic glaze.
3. Place in a single layer on large, rimmed baking sheet. Bake 20 to 25 minutes, stirring halfway through, or until tender.
4. Finish with a drizzle of balsamic glaze, as desired.

SPAM® Musubi Pizza

⏱ **TIME:** 30 MINUTES   🍴 **YIELD:** 4 SERVINGS

You'll want a second slice of sizzle after trying this SPAM® musubi pizza. Featuring a nori crust, this pizza is topped with the classic musubi favorite flavors of furikake, teriyaki sauce, SPAM® Classic, kimchi, and more.

INGREDIENTS

- 1 (12-ounce) can SPAM® Classic, sliced into 8 slices
- 3 cups cooked sushi rice
- 8 sheets nori
- Suggested toppings: Browned SPAM® Classic rounds, furikake and teriyaki sauce, browned SPAM® Classic pieces, chopped kimchi, green onions, and togarashi.

DIRECTIONS

1. Using 1½-inch cookie cutter, cut 2 slices SPAM® Classic into rounds. Dice 2 slices SPAM® Classic.

2. In large skillet over medium-high heat, cook SPAM® Classic slices, rounds, and diced pieces 3 to 5 minutes or until well browned. Remove from skillet. Cut slices into 4 strips each.

3. Spread layer of rice over 1 nori, leaving 1-inch border at top. Place 4 strips

SPAM® Classic just below the middle of the rice. Roll like a sushi roll to form the "pizza crust."

4. Cut 1 nori into triangle shape to form the base of the pizza slice. On serving plate, place the sushi roll crust on top of the triangle. Spread thin layer of rice over the triangle. Top pizza slice with SPAM® Classic rounds and diced pieces and suggested toppings. Repeat to make 4 slices.

SPAM® Pizza Casserole

🕐 **TIME:** 40 MINUTES   🍴 **YIELD:** 8 SERVINGS

When zoo animals get hungry, you tame them with food to keep them happy. Same with teens. When they get hungry, throw some of this zesty, satisfying casserole their way. Otherwise, those wild, ravenous beasts are going to turn your kitchen into a zoo.

INGREDIENTS

- 6 cups frozen shredded hash brown potatoes, thawed
- 1 (10.75-ounce) can Cheddar cheese soup
- 1 large egg, lightly beaten
- ½ teaspoon salt
- 1/4 teaspoon pepper
- 1 tablespoon vegetable oil
- 2 (12-ounce) cans SPAM® Oven Roasted Turkey, cut into ½-inch cubes
- 1 onion, chopped
- 1 (4-ounce) can mushroom stems and pieces, drained
- 1 (14- to 16-ounce) jar pizza sauce
- 4 cups shredded pizza cheese blend

DIRECTIONS

1. Heat oven to 400°F. Grease a 15x10x1-inch baking pan.

2. In a medium bowl, combine the potatoes, soup, egg, salt, and pepper; mix well. Spread the mixture evenly in the baking pan. Bake for 20 to 22 minutes or until lightly browned.

3. Meanwhile, in a large skillet, heat oil over medium heat. Add the SPAM® Oven Roasted Turkey, onion, and mushrooms. Cook for 5 to 8 minutes or until lightly browned.

4. Stir in pizza sauce.

5. Sprinkle hot potato crust with 2 cups cheese. Top with SPAM® mixture and remaining 2 cups cheese. Bake for 5 to 7 minutes or until cheese is melted.

6. Cut the pizza into squares.

SPAM® Kimchi Fried Rice

 TIME: 30 MINUTES   **YIELD:** 4 SERVINGS

 This satisfying fried rice is not the high-heat stir-fry you might expect, featuring cubes of SPAM® Less Sodium, kimchi, gochujang paste, and sesame seeds. A bowlful of this fried rice recipe accompanied by a fried egg is a delicious Korean-inspired quick meal.

INGREDIENTS

- 1 (12-ounce) can SPAM® Less Sodium, diced
- 2 teaspoons vegetable oil
- 1 cup chopped kimchi
- 3 cups cooked rice
- ¼ cup water
- 2 tablespoons kimchi juice
- 2 tablespoons gochujang paste
- 1 tablespoon toasted sesame seed oil
- 1 green onion, chopped
- 1 sheet roasted gim, shredded
- 1 tablespoon roasted sesame seeds
- 4 fried eggs, if desired

DIRECTIONS

1. In large skillet over medium-high heat, cook SPAM® Less Sodium 3 to 5 minutes, or until lightly browned and crisped. Remove from skillet.

2. In same skillet, heat vegetable oil. Add kimchi. Stir-fry 1 minute. Add rice, water, kimchi juice, and gochujang. Stir-fry 5 to 7 minutes.

3. Add sesame oil and remove from heat.

4. Sprinkle with chopped green onion, roasted gim, and sesame seeds. Serve topped with eggs, if desired.

Surf and Turf SPAM® Musubi

 TIME: 50 MINUTES   **YIELD:** 4–8 SERVINGS

Sizzled slices of SPAM® Classic are wrapped up in a bed of nori with shrimp tempura, spring greens, Sriracha mayo, and sushi rice. Elevate it to an unforgettable experience with a topping of edible gold leaf!

INGREDIENTS

- 1 (12-ounce) can SPAM® Classic, sliced into 8 slices
- 8 eggs, beaten
- 4 sheets nori, cut in half
- 4 cups cooked sushi rice
- 1 cup mixed spring greens
- 8 frozen shrimp tempura, cooked according to package directions
- Edible gold leaf, as desired

SRIRACHA MAYONNAISE

- ½ cup kewpie Japanese mayonnaise
- 2 tablespoons sriracha sauce

DIRECTIONS

1. In large, nonstick skillet over medium-high heat, cook SPAM® Classic slices 3 to 4 minutes, or until browned. Remove from pan.

2. In same skillet, pour in half of the eggs. Cook 45 seconds; lift edge of egg with spatula to allow uncooked portion to flow underneath 2 to 3 minutes or until egg is set. Fold up. Cut into 4 sections.

3. Repeat process with remaining eggs to have 8 folded egg portions.

4. To make sriracha mayonnaise, combine kewpie Japanese mayonnaise and sriracha sauce in a small bowl.

5. On work surface, place half nori sheet. Using wet fingers, spread one end with rice to ½-inch thickness. Top with a spoonful of sriracha mayonnaise.

6. Layer one SPAM® Classic slice, one egg portion, a few leaves mixed spring greens, and 1 shrimp tempura. Spread rice on other end of nori sheet. Fold to close as a sandwich. Top with edible gold leaf.

Desserts

150 Maple Brown Sugar SPAM® Ice Cream

152 SPAM® Pineapple Cheesecake

SPAM® Pineapple
Cheesecake

Maple Brown Sugar SPAM® Ice Cream

 TIME: 1 HOURS, 20 MINUTES   **YIELD:** 8 SERVINGS

You've heard of savory ice cream. Now try SPAM® ice cream! This favorite State Fair recipe will satisfy that sweet tooth, with delicious SPAM® with Real HORMEL® Bacon candied with brown sugar, maple syrup, and vanilla!

INGREDIENTS

- 1 (12 ounce) can SPAM® with Real HORMEL® Bacon
- ½ cup brown sugar
- ½ cup real maple syrup
- 1 teaspoon vanilla extract
- 2 cups heavy cream
- 2 cups milk
- 2 teaspoons bourbon vanilla
- Pinch salt
- ¾ cup granulated sugar

DIRECTIONS

1. Dice the SPAM® with Real HORMEL® Bacon into ¼-inch cubes. Place in a large skillet with brown sugar, maple syrup, and vanilla.

2. Cook over medium heat until bubbly; reduce heat and stir until the sauce is reduced by about one-third. Allow the SPAM® mixture to cool.

3. In mixing bowl, combine cream, milk, bourbon vanilla, and salt. Add sugar and stir until dissolved.

4. Place the cream mixture into an ice cream maker and follow the manufacturer's instructions for freezing. As the mixture finishes freezing and is still soft, pour into storage container.

5. Freeze ice cream for about an hour, and then fold in the SPAM® mixture, just swirling it into the ice cream. **Do not overmix!**

6. Place in freezer to harden. Serves 8.

SPAM® Pineapple Cheesecake

 TIME: 3 HOURS, 15 MINUTES   **YIELD:** 24 SERVINGS

 This unexpectedly unique recipe brings a savory twist on the classic cheesecake dessert. This culinary creation features a delectable oyster cracker and Parmesan crust embracing a luscious filling of diced SPAM® Classic, cream cheese, eggs, pineapple tidbits, Swiss cheese, chives, basil, and a medley of spices, all baked to perfection. This cheesecake is a savory sensation that pairs perfectly with assorted crackers as dip or can be served in slices like the traditional dessert.

INGREDIENTS

CRUST

- 3 cups oyster crackers, crushed
- 1 cup Parmesan cheese, grated
- ⅓ cup butter, melted

FILLING

- 1 (12-ounce) can SPAM® Classic, diced
- 4 (8-ounce) packages cream cheese, softened
- 4 eggs, lightly beaten
- 1 (8-ounce) can pineapple tidbits in juice, drained
- 2 cups shredded Swiss cheese
- ⅓ cup chives, minced
- ¼ cup fresh basil, minced
- ¼ teaspoon salt
- ¼ teaspoon white pepper
- ¼ teaspoon garlic powder
- Assorted crackers

DIRECTIONS

1. In a bowl, combine the oyster cracker crumbs, Parmesan cheese, and butter; then set aside ¼ cup for the topping.

2. Press the remaining crumb mixture onto the bottom and inches up the sides of a greased 9-inch springform pan. Cover and refrigerate for at least 30 minutes.

3. Meanwhile, in a skillet, heat the SPAM® Classic until lightly browned, and then set aside.

4. In a large mixing bowl, beat the cream cheese until smooth. Add eggs; beat on low until just combined.

5. Add the SPAM® Classic, pineapple, cheese, chives, basil, salt, pepper, and garlic powder. Beat until just combined, then pour into crust and sprinkle with the reserved crumb mixture.

6. Place the pan on a baking sheet. Bake at 325°F for 70 to 90 minutes or until the filling is almost set, and then turn the oven off. Leave the cheesecake in the oven with the door ajar for 30 minutes.

7. Cool on a wire rack for 10 minutes. Carefully run a knife around the edge of the pan to loosen.

8. Cool the cheesecake for 1 additional hour. Remove the cheesecake from the pan and refrigerate overnight, if serving chilled. Also great served warm or at room temperature. Serve with assorted crackers. Makes 24 to 36 servings.

From Chefs' Kitchens to Yours

Chefs from all over the world are embracing the versatility of SPAM® products in their dishes. From high-end, gourmet restaurants to fun, kitschy food trucks, you'll find SPAM® products on the menu. This chapter includes all kinds of traditional and quirky recipes, collected straight from international chefs' kitchens!

156 Sprunch

158 SPAM® Horizons Bagel

159 SPAM® Classic with Red Beans and Rice

160 SPAM® Corn Dogs

162 SPAM® Scotch Egg

164 SPAM® Pesto-Stuffed Peppers

165 Mini SPAM® Quiche

166 Country Fried Chicken and Biscuits with SPAM® Classic Gravy

168 Curried SPAM® Pot Stickers with Coconut Pineapple Sauce

170 SPAM® Shakshuka

172 Bulgogi SPAM® Bao Buns with Gochujang Slaw

174 SPAM® Benedict with Kimchi and BimBim Hollandaise

176 Grilled SPAM® Shady

177 Hong Kong-Style SPAM® Classic and Egg Macaroni Soup

178 Crystal Wrap SPAM® Classic

180 SPAM® Rice Pancake

181 Wonton SPAM® Eggroll

182 Wisconsin SPAM® Pierogi

184 Fried Jalapeño SPAM® Poppers

186 Deviled SPAM® Grilled Cheese

187 SPAM® Reuben Rollups

188 Fried Egg SPAM®wich

190 Sweet and Tangy Asian SPAM® Sandwich

191 Cheesy Tomato SPAM®wiches

192 SPAM® and Breakfast Ramen

194 SIR CAN-A-LOT™ Sandwich

SPAM® Corn Dogs

Sprunch

SUBMITTED BY BETH ESPOSITO, CHEF/OWNER OF PINK GARLIC, TV PERSONALITY, AND FOOD CONCEPT CREATOR
FACEBOOK: PINK GARLIC | INSTAGRAM: @CHEFBETH01 | X: @PINKGARLICBETH

🕐 **TIME:** 25 MINUTES   🍽 **YIELD:** 1 SERVING

Get brunch ready with this colossal concoction of deliciousness! Take the classic batter-dipped sandwich and turn it into a delectable SPAM® brand duo: SPAM® Classic and SPAM® Oven Roasted Turkey. Sticky, savory, and sweet is what this sammie is all about. Open wide because this is a mouthful!

INGREDIENTS

- 2 slices 1½-inch thick cut challah
- 2 extra large eggs
- 2 tablespoons heavy cream
- ⅓ teaspoon ground cinnamon
- Dash each nutmeg, sea salt, powdered onion, powdered garlic
- 1 teaspoon vanilla
- ⅓ cup vegetable oil
- 4 ounces SPAM® Classic sliced thin (on slicer or by hand)
- 4 ounces SPAM® Oven Roasted Turkey sliced thin (on slicer or by hand)
- 3 ounces raclette cheese (shred or slice thin by hand)
- ⅓ cup whole cranberry sauce or use your favorite prepared product
- 1 tablespoon mayonnaise
- 1 cup maple syrup
- Dash liquid smoke
- 1 sprig fresh rosemary
- Garnish with cornichons (optional)

DIRECTIONS

1. Add a sprig of fresh rosemary and liquid smoke to the syrup and set aside.
2. Mix together the cranberry sauce and mayonnaise and set aside.
3. Whisk together eggs, cream, vanilla, cinnamon, nutmeg, and salt.
4. Warm a cast iron flattop griddle or large pan to medium heat.
5. Drizzle half the oil on the griddle. Dip the bread into the egg mixture and cook on both sides until lightly browned but cooked through.
6. Add the remaining portion of oil on the griddle, add SPAM® Classic and SPAM® Oven Roasted Turkey separately, and cook until brown around the edges. Set aside.
7. To build your sandwich, start with one slice of the battered bread, and smear on the cranberry mixture. Add SPAM® Classic and sprinkle on raclette cheese. Next add SPAM® Oven Roasted Turkey and top with another slice of battered bread. Drizzle with rosemary syrup and enjoy!

HOMEMADE CRANBERRY SAUCE

INGREDIENTS

- 1 cup whole fresh cranberries
- 1 cup light brown sugar
- 1 teaspoon vanilla
- 1 flower of star anise
- 1 small sprig rosemary
- Dash salt

DIRECTIONS

Add all ingredients in pot on low heat and cook until it thickens. As the mixture cools, it will get as thick as jelly.

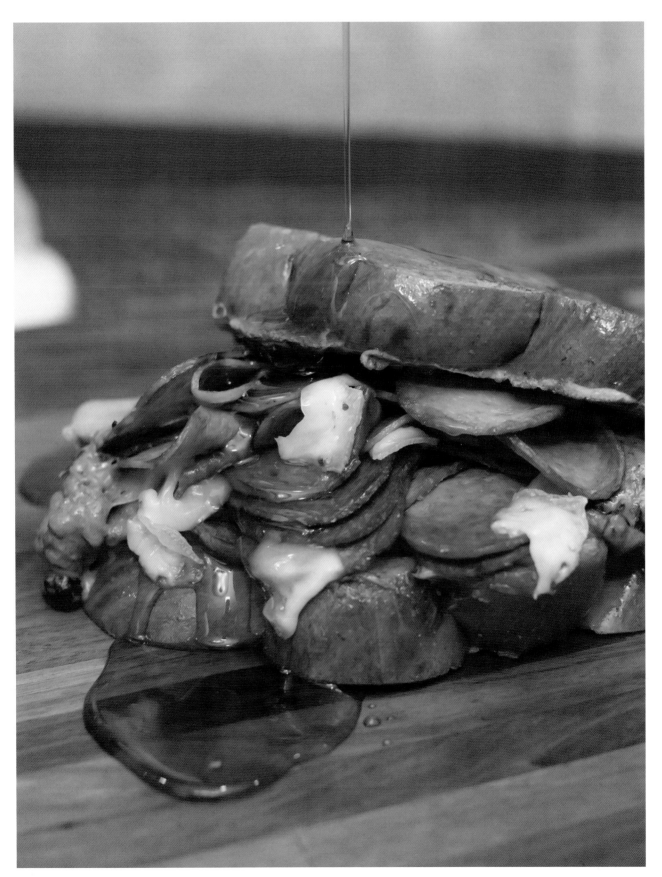

SPAM® Horizons Bagel

SUBMITTED BY BETH ESPOSITO, CHEF/OWNER OF PINK GARLIC, TV PERSONALITY, AND FOOD CONCEPT CREATOR
FACEBOOK: PINK GARLIC | INSTAGRAM: @CHEFBETH01 | X: @PINKGARLICBETH

🕐 **TIME:** 15 MINUTES   🍽 **YIELD:** 1 SERVING

 Let this ray of sunshine wake up your senses for a light and flavor-filling snack. Make an average bagel completely unconventional by pairing with fruits, nuts, and the savory goodness of the original SPAM® Classic. A simple and easy way to start your day.

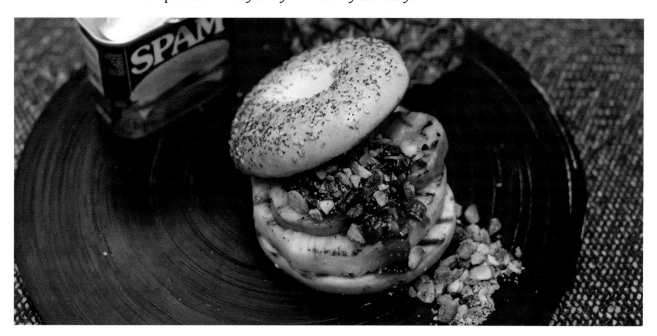

INGREDIENTS

- 1 everything bagel (or bagel of choice)
- 2 slices SPAM® Classic
- 1 tablespoon salted butter, room temperature
- 1 slice fresh pineapple, sliced round at 1-inch thick, core removed
- Dash of ground allspice
- Fresh basil leaf
- 2 tablespoons fig jam
- 1 tablespoon chopped, salted pistachios

DIRECTIONS

1. Slice the bagel in half.
2. Smear the butter on both sides of the bagel and set aside.
3. Shred the basil leaf, mix it with the fig jam, and set aside.
4. Sprinkle the allspice onto the pineapple round and set aside.
5. On a grill or cast-iron grill pan, sear the slice of pineapple, 2 slices of SPAM® Classic, and buttered bagel.
6. Chop the pistachios and set aside.
7. To build the bagel, start from bottom slice of the bagel, add the pineapple, slices of SPAM® Classic, dollop of the basil-fig jam, sprinkle crushed pistachios, and top with the other half of the bagel. Then see the sunshine!

SPAM® Classic with Red Beans and Rice

SUBMITTED BY CHRISTIAN GILL, *GUY'S GROCERY GAMES* CHAMPION,
EXECUTIVE CHEF OF BOOMTOWN BISCUITS AND WHISKEY, CINCINNATI, OHIO

 TIME: 30 MINUTES   **YIELD:** 6 SERVINGS

 Wake up your taste buds and make them smile with this hearty dish. The Creole influence will add some literal spice to your life!

INGREDIENTS

- 1 can SPAM® Classic (diced)
- 2 (15-ounce) cans dark red kidney beans
- 1 large white onion (large dice)
- 2 serrano peppers (thinly sliced)
- 1 large green bell pepper (large dice)
- 4 cloves of garlic (minced)
- 2 stalks of celery (diced)
- 2 tablespoons chopped curly parsley
- 2 tablespoons butter
- 2 teaspoons creole seasoning
- 2 cups cooked jasmine rice

CREOLE SEASONING

- 2 teaspoons chili powder
- 2 teaspoons salt
- 1 teaspoon garlic powder
- 1 teaspoon onion powder
- 1 teaspoon paprika
- 1 teaspoon dried thyme
- 1 teaspoon cayenne
- 1 teaspoon black pepper
- 1 teaspoon oregano

DIRECTIONS

1. In a large skillet over high heat, sear diced SPAM® Classic until browned and crispy on all sides.
2. Add butter to the skillet and melt.
3. Once butter is melted, add diced onion, bell pepper, garlic, and celery to the skillet and sauté for 5 minutes or until vegetables soften and the aroma of garlic builds.
4. Once SPAM® Classic and the vegetables are cooked, add creole seasoning and 2 cans of dark red kidney beans with the liquid from the cans.
5. Bring the contents of the skillet to a boil, and then simmer for 10 minutes, stirring occasionally.
6. Serve with a side of hot jasmine rice and garnish with coarsely chopped parsley.

SPAM® Corn Dogs

SUBMITTED BY JONATHAN MELENDEZ, FOOD PHOTOGRAPHER AND BLOGGER, FOUNDER OF THE CANDID APPETITE
INSTAGRAM: @JONJON33 | JONATHANMELENDEZ.COM

 TIME: 30 MINUTES   **YIELD:** 12 SERVINGS

 These SPAM® Corn Dogs are a fun take on a carnival classic! Perfect for appetizers, snacks, or even a fun weekend or weekday lunch. Keep them in the freezer and just rewarm in the oven whenever you're in need of a delicious treat!

INGREDIENTS

- 1¼ cups all-purpose flour, divided
- ¾ cup yellow cornmeal
- 1½ teaspoons baking powder
- 1 teaspoon granulated sugar
- ¾ teaspoon salt
- ¾ cup plus 2 tablespoons buttermilk
- 2 large eggs
- 2 (12-ounce) cans SPAM® Less Sodium
- Vegetable oil for frying
- Ketchup, for serving
- Mustard, for serving

DIRECTIONS

1. In a large bowl whisk together cup of the flour, cornmeal, sugar, baking powder, and salt. Pour in the buttermilk and lightly beaten eggs. Mix until evenly combined and smooth. Pour into a tall drinking glass and set aside.

2. Cut the SPAM® Less Sodium into twelve even logs. Skewer the logs with a thin popsicle stick. Dredge the skewered SPAM® logs in flour and dust to shake excess. Then, working with one at a time, dip into the glass filled with the corn batter. Lift and dunk again to fully coat.

3. Fill a large pot halfway up vegetable oil and heat to 360°F, monitoring it with a deep-fry or candy thermometer.

4. Once hot, carefully lay the coated corn dogs into the hot oil. Cook about three at a time so you don't overcrowd the pot. Fry until golden brown all around, about 4 to 6 minutes, turning halfway. Drain excess oil with a slotted spoon or a pair of thongs. Place on a plate lined with paper towels to catch grease. Transfer to a wire rack placed over a baking sheet. Continue frying until all the corn dogs are cooked. Place the baking sheet in the oven to rewarm and get them crispy before eating.

5. Serve with mustard and ketchup on the side for dunking. Enjoy!

SPAM® Scotch Egg

SUBMITTED BY CHRISTY GOODE, CHEF, NORTH WALES, UK
INSTAGRAM: @CHRISTYGOODE91

 TIME: 1 HOUR   **YIELD:** 2 SERVINGS

 Calling all lads and lasses! So the Scotch egg may not truly be Scottish, but it truly is a delight to eat! Enjoy this traditional UK dish with a SPAM® Classic twist.

INGREDIENTS

FOR THE SCOTCH EGG

- 1 (7-ounce) can SPAM® Classic, chopped
- 7 ounces minced pork
- 2 tablespoons all-purpose flour
- 3 eggs
- ¼ cup panko breadcrumbs
- ½ teaspoon cracked black pepper

FOR THE RED PEPPER CHUTNEY

- 3 large red bell peppers
- 4 tablespoons olive oil
- 2 fluid ounces balsamic vinegar
- ¼ cup demerara sugar

FOR THE CARAMELIZED PINEAPPLE

- ½ of 1 fresh pineapple
- 2 tablespoons demerara sugar
- 1½ tablespoons orange juice

DIRECTIONS

FOR THE SCOTCH EGGS:

1. Place 2 of the eggs into boiling water for 6 minutes, then remove and place in iced water.
2. While the eggs are cooling, place chopped SPAM® Classic and pork mince into food processor. Season with black pepper then pulse to combine the mixture.
3. Once the eggs are cool, remove them from iced water and peel the shell from the egg.
4. Take the sausage and SPAM® Classic mixture and form around the egg. Once the mixture is formed around the eggs, roll them in flour, then dip them into the beaten egg, then into the panko breadcrumbs.
5. Fry until they are golden brown. Then bake them for 7 minutes.

FOR THE RED PEPPER CHUTNEY:

1. Dice the red pepper and place into a pan with the olive oil. Cook on medium heat for 5 minutes until soft.
2. Reduce the heat, and add the balsamic vinegar and demerara sugar. Cook on low heat, stirring occasionally for 25 minutes.
3. Remove from the heat and cool in the fridge.

FOR THE CARAMELIZED PINEAPPLE:

1. Cut the pineapple into small rectangles. Place them in a pot and simmer in the orange juice on medium heat for 15 minutes or until soft.
2. Add the demerara sugar and cook on medium to high heat for 5 more minutes to caramelize.

SPAM® Pesto-Stuffed Peppers

SUBMITTED BY CINDY KERSCHNER, AWARD-WINNING CHEF AND FOOD SPORT COMPETITOR
FACEBOOK: CINDYSRECIPESANDWRITINGS | INSTAGRAM: @CINDYKERSCHNER | | X: @WRITELANE
WWW.PINTEREST.COM/CINDYKERSCHNER | WWW.CINDYSRECIPESANDWRITINGS.COM

 TIME: 35 MINUTES   **YIELD:** 2 SERVINGS

 SPAM® Pesto-Stuffed Peppers serve garlicy pesto-tossed SPAM® Classic, basmati rice, and spinach piled high in tender baked bell peppers. Topped with shaved Parmesan cheese, gently melted.

INGREDIENTS

- 2 medium-sized bell peppers, tops removed and seeded
- 4 ounces SPAM® Classic, diced
- 1 cup basmati, jasmine, or long grain rice, cooked
- 1 cup fresh baby spinach
- ½ cup fresh basil
- 2 cloves garlic
- ¼ cup grated Parmesan cheese, plus 2 tablespoons
- 1/4 cup olive oil

DIRECTIONS

1. Preheat oven to 350°F.

2. In a medium-sized saucepan, add peppers and tops with enough water to cover it. Bring to a boil. Reduce heat to medium and blanch peppers and tops approximately 4 to 5 minutes until soft but not mushy. Remove peppers and tops from water. Add spinach to leftover hot water and wilt spinach for about 1 minute. Remove spinach, drain, and chop.

3. Place basil, garlic, and ¼ cup Parmesan cheese in a food processor. Chop to form a paste, approximately 1 minute. Drizzle in olive oil while processor is running. Set blended pesto aside.

4. In a medium-sized bowl, mix SPAM® Classic, rice, spinach, and pesto. Loosely stuff peppers. Place stuffed peppers in a shallow baking dish. Sprinkle with remaining grated Parmesan. Bake at 350°F, uncovered, for about 15 minutes until thoroughly heated.

Mini SPAM® Quiche

SUBMITTED BY DENISE DE CASTRO, PMP
INSTAGRAM: @DEECUISINE | WWW.DEECUISINE.COM

 TIME: 1 HOUR   **YIELD:** 4 SERVINGS

 These Mini SPAM® Quiches are easy to make and so delicious! Phyllo dough shells can be found in the freezer aisle of your grocery store. These mini quiches are perfect to serve as an appetizer or with a salad for Sunday brunch.

INGREDIENTS

- 12 mini phyllo shells
- 4 ounces diced SPAM® Less Sodium
- 3 large eggs
- ½ cup milk
- ½ cup shredded Cheddar cheese
- 1 scallion, thinly sliced—separate the white base from the green leaves
- 1 teaspoon olive oil
- Salt and pepper, to taste

DIRECTIONS

1. Preheat oven to 350°F.
2. Line a baking sheet with parchment paper and place thawed phyllo dough shells on it.
3. Heat olive oil in a pan over medium heat.
4. Add white parts of the scallion and sauté until translucent, about 2 to 3 minutes.
5. Add diced SPAM® Less Sodium to the pan and cook for 5 minutes, stirring occasionally.
6. Transfer to a paper towel-lined plate.
7. Spoon evenly into phyllo dough shells. Top with shredded Cheddar cheese and scallion greens.
8. In a mixing bowl, whisk together eggs and milk. Season with salt and pepper. Fill each shell with egg mixture.
9. Bake for 15 minutes until the eggs are puffy.

Country Fried Chicken and Biscuits with SPAM® Classic Gravy

SUBMITTED BY GEORGEANN LEAMING, *CHOPPED* CHAMPION, CHEF DE CUISINE AT R2L RESTAURANT, PHILADELPHIA, PENNSYLVANIA
#CHOPPEDCHAMPION | FACEBOOK: CHEFGEORGEANNLEAMING | INSTAGRAM: @GEORGEANN_LEAMING

TIME: 1 HOUR, 10 MINUTES   **YIELD:** 4-6 SERVINGS

Step up your brunch game with this dish! What can be better than delicious fried chicken sitting on top of warm, fluffy biscuits draped with a creamy sauce made with SPAM® Classic? This new twist on a favorite dish will have everyone asking for that extra ladle of gravy!

INGREDIENTS

- 4 boneless, skinless chicken thighs, cut in half

FOR THE SEASONED FLOUR
- 2 cups flour
- 1 tablespoon kosher salt
- 1 teaspoon black pepper
- 2 teaspoons granulated garlic
- 2 teaspoons granulated onion
- 1 teaspoon paprika

FOR THE CHICKEN MARINADE
- 1 quart buttermilk
- 1 tablespoon hot sauce
- 1 tablespoon kosher salt
- 1 teaspoon black pepper
- 1 teaspoon ground thyme
- 1 teaspoon paprika

FOR THE BISCUITS
- 2 cups flour
- 2 tablespoons baking powder

- 1 teaspoon baking soda
- 1 teaspoon kosher salt
- cup butter, cubed

FOR THE GRAVY
- 2 tablespoons oil
- 1 can SPAM® Classic
- cup sweet onion, small diced
- 1 tablespoon flour
- 2 cups heavy cream
- 2 teaspoons black pepper
- Salt to taste

DIRECTIONS

BISCUITS

1. Preheat oven to 400°F. Add biscuit ingredients to a food processor and pulse until butter becomes pea sized.

2. Transfer the mix to a bowl and add 1 cup buttermilk. Stir to combine. Lightly knead with hands until dough comes together. Dough should be slightly tacky. Add more flour if too wet, or add more milk if too dry. Flour the work surface and lay dough on top. Using hands, press dough until ½-inch thick. Cut into 3-inch circles using a cutter or a glass. Refold excess dough until used up.

3. Line a sheet pan with parchment paper and place biscuits on the pan. Beat an egg with 1 tablespoon of water. Use a pastry brush and brush egg wash onto the tops of the biscuits. Bake until golden brown.

CHICKEN

1. Preheat fryer or pot with about 1 inch of oil to 350°F. In a medium mixing bowl combine flour, kosher salt, black pepper, garlic, onion, and paprika.

2. Dredge the chicken pieces in the seasoned flour. Return to the marinade to moisten again and then back into the flour. Set on a baking rack while finishing the remainder of the pieces.

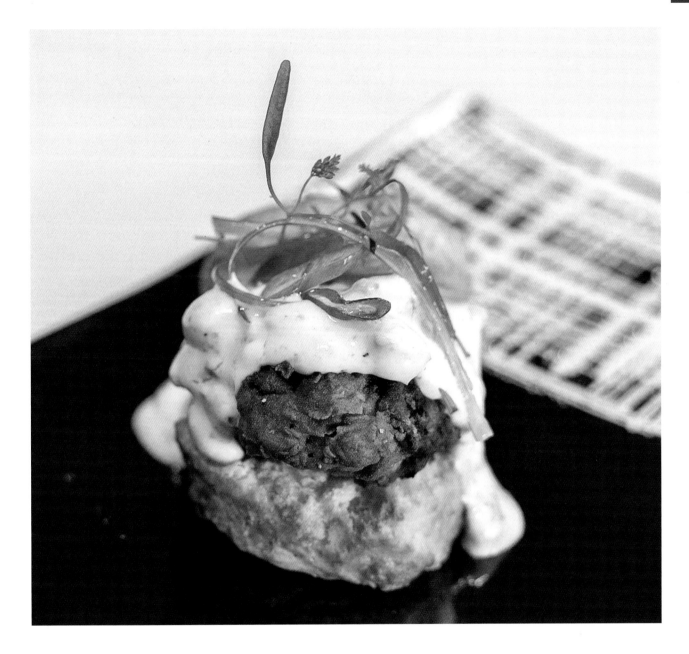

3. Fry each piece until golden brown and a thermometer inserted into chicken reads 180°F. Place the pieces on a clean baking rack over a sheet pan and keep warm in low oven until ready to assemble.

GRAVY

1. Heat oil in a pot over medium-high heat. Pulse SPAM® Classic in a food processor or dice into small pieces. Add SPAM® Classic to hot pan and occasionally stir until browned.

4. Add onions and sauté for 1 minute. Lower the heat and add the flour. Stir to incorporate. Slowly whisk in the milk and bring to a simmer. Allow to cook for 10 minutes to cook the flour out, stirring occasionally. Season with salt and pepper.

ASSEMBLY

1. Split the biscuits in half and place the fried chicken on them. Top with the SPAM® Classic gravy. Garnish with some sliced scallions, if desired. Serve warm.

Curried SPAM® Pot Stickers with Coconut Pineapple Sauce

SUBMITTED BY GEORGEANN LEAMING, *CHOPPED* CHAMPION, CHEF DE CUISINE AT R2L RESTAURANT, PHILADELPHIA, PENNSYLVANIA
FACEBOOK: CHEFGEORGEANNLEAMING | INSTAGRAM: @GEORGEANN_LEAMING

 TIME: 1 HOUR   **YIELD:** 4 SERVINGS

 A little package full of flavor! Spicy meets sweet in these savory pot stickers. The tender, steamed dough offers a crispy bottom and flavor-filled stuffing. The coconut pineapple sauce is a quick yet tasty sauce that you will want to whip up for more than these pot stickers!

INGREDIENTS

FOR FILLING

- 1 can SPAM® Classic, cut into small chunks
- 2 tablespoons heavy cream
- ¼ cup yellow curry paste (choose red paste for hotter filling)*
- 2 tablespoons cilantro leaves
- 1 small carrot, small diced
- 2 tablespoons yellow raisins, soaked in hot water for 5 minutes, drained and rough chopped
- 1 pack round dumpling wrappers*
- 1 teaspoon cornstarch mixed into 3 tablespoons water

FOR THE SAUCE

- 1 cup unsweetened coconut milk
- 1 teaspoon turmeric
- 1 can crushed pineapple, juice drained and reserved
- 2 teaspoons cornstarch
- Salt to taste
- Cilantro and scallions for garnish

DIRECTIONS

1. In a food processor, pulse the SPAM® Classic until it's in small pieces. Add cream and curry and pulse to combine.

2. Place in a small bowl and mix in carrots and raisins.

3. Lay out two or three dumpling wrappers at a time and leave the others covered with plastic wrap to prevent drying out. Place about 1 teaspoon of mixture into the center of each wrapper. Using your finger, wipe some of the cornstarch mix around the edge of the wrapper. Bring the sides up around the filling, leaving the bottom flat. Pinch together or fold into several pleats, making sure they are sealed. Add more cornstarch mixture as needed to close them.

4. For the sauce, heat coconut milk in a small pot over medium heat until just simmering. Add the turmeric and ¼ cup of the crushed pineapple. Use ¼ cup of the reserved pineapple juice to whisk in the cornstarch. Add the mix to the simmering coconut milk and whisk to combine. Season with salt. Set aside.

5. To cook dumplings as pot stickers: heat a small amount of oil in a deep sauté pan over medium high heat. Place dumplings in a pan. Do not overcrowd the pan. Brown the bottoms then add ½ cup water to the pan and cover with a tight lid. Allow to steam for a few minutes then remove lid and allow water to fully cook off. Allow the bottoms to crisp. Remove from the pan and repeat the process until all the dumplings are cooked, keeping cooked dumplings covered to stay warm.

6. Alternatively, if you would like crispy fried dumplings, simply fry in a fryer or a pot with oil at 350°F until golden brown.

7. To serve, smear some of the pineapple sauce onto a plate or platter and place the dumpling along the side of the sauce. Place some of the leftover crushed pineapple on the plate as well, if desired. Top with hand-torn cilantro leaves and sliced scallions, both white and green parts.

* *Wrappers and curry paste can be found at an Asian market or some specialty grocery stores.*

SPAM® Shakshuka

SUBMITTED BY JONATHAN MELENDEZ, FOOD PHOTOGRAPHER AND BLOGGER, FOUNDER OF *THE CANDID APPETITE*
INSTAGRAM: @JONJON33 | JONATHANMELENDEZ.COM

 TIME: 45 MINUTES   **YIELD:** 4 SERVINGS

 This traditional North African dish is composed of eggs cooked in a slightly spicy tomato sauce. It's the perfect quick and easy dish that you can make for breakfast, brunch, or even a simple dinner. It is studded with crispy SPAM® Less Sodium, and it will be the highlight to any meal.

INGREDIENTS

- 2 tablespoons olive oil
- 1 (12-ounce) can SPAM® Less Sodium, diced
- 1 small red onion, diced
- 1 medium red bell pepper, diced
- 2 garlic cloves, minced
- 1 teaspoon ground cumin
- 1 teaspoon paprika

- 1 teaspoon dried oregano
- ¼ teaspoon cayenne pepper
- ¼ teaspoon crushed red pepper flakes (optional)
- 1 tablespoon tomato paste
- 1 (28-ounce) can whole tomatoes with their juices
- ¾ teaspoon Kosher salt

- ¼ teaspoon fresh cracked black pepper
- 8 large eggs
- ½ cup crumbled feta cheese
- ¼ cup fresh cilantro leaves
- ¼ cup fresh parsley leaves

DIRECTIONS

1. Set a large skillet over medium-high heat. Once hot, drizzle in the olive oil and add the diced SPAM® Less Sodium.

2. Cook, stirring often, until brown and crispy, about 4 to 5 minutes. Using a slotted spoon, remove the SPAM® Less Sodium to a plate and set aside.

3. Add the onion, red bell pepper, and garlic to the skillet and cook until softened, about 8 minutes. Stir in the cumin, paprika, oregano, cayenne, red pepper flakes (if using), and the tomato paste. Allow to cook for about a minute to develop their flavors.

4. Add the whole tomatoes with their juices, and break them up with a wooden spoon. Season with salt and pepper and simmer until the sauce has thickened, about 10 minutes.

5. Gently crack the eggs into the skillet over the tomatoes. Season the eggs with salt and pepper and cover the skillet with a lid. Cook over moderate heat until the egg whites have just set, 10 to 12 minutes.

6. Turn off the flame, uncover and top the shakshuka with feta, cilantro, and parsley before serving.

Bulgogi SPAM® Bao Buns with Gochujang Slaw

SUBMITTED BY GEORGEANN LEAMING, *CHOPPED* CHAMPION, CHEF DE CUISINE AT R2L RESTAURANT, PHILADELPHIA, PENNSYLVANIA
FACEBOOK: CHEFGEORGEANNLEAMING | INSTAGRAM: @GEORGEANN_LEAMING

 TIME: 45 MINUTES   **YIELD:** 4-6 SERVINGS

 A Korean-inspired dish that is a great party snack or quick dinner idea. The bulgogi marinade provides a sweet, crunchy sear that is paired with a bit of spice from the gochujang slaw. Sure to become one of your go-to recipes!

INGREDIENTS

FOR THE MARINADE

- 2 tablespoons light brown sugar
- 1 ripe pear, peeled, cored, medium diced
- ¼ cup soy sauce
- 1 teaspoon sesame oil
- 3 cloves garlic
- 3-inch piece fresh ginger, peeled and chopped
- 2 tablespoons oil
- 2 scallions sliced thin, white parts (reserve green part for below)

FOR THE SLAW

- 1 small head Napa cabbage, sliced thin (about 2 cups)
- ½ cup shredded carrots
- Sliced green parts of the 2 scallions from above
- 1 teaspoon gochujang paste (Korean pepper paste)
- ¼ cup Kewpie mayo (regular mayo may be substituted)
- 1 tablespoon chopped cilantro leaves
- 1 teaspoon black sesame seeds
- Salt to taste
- 1 can SPAM® Classic
- 1 package plain bao buns*

DIRECTIONS

1. In a small mixing bowl, whisk marinade ingredients to combine. Slice the SPAM® Classic lengthwise into ¼-inch slices. Cut each slice again into ¼-inch-thick slices to make (julienne) strips. Add the strips into the marinade and allow to sit for at least half hour, or up to 2 hours.

2. In another bowl, mix slaw ingredients, seasoning with salt to taste. For a spicier slaw, add more gochujang or less for mild.

3. Warm the bao buns in a steamer basket over of pot of simmering water or in a microwave, wrapped in damp paper towels.

4. In a large nonstick skillet, heat 1 tablespoon of oil over medium high heat. Add the marinated SPAM® Classic and allow to brown on the first side then turn and cook until all sides have browned. (The browning will be darker due to sugars caramelizing; this is a good and tasty thing!)

5. Place SPAM® slices into warmed bao buns. Top with slaw mixture. Add additional cilantro and scallions for garnish, if desired.

Buns may be found at an Asian market or online.

SPAM® Benedict with Kimchi and BimBim Hollandaise

SUBMITTED BY KEVIN HICKEY, CHEF AT THE DUCK INN, CHICAGO, ILLINOIS
FACEBOOK: DUCKINNCHICAGO | INSTAGRAM: @DUCKINNCHICAGO | X: @DUCKINNCHICAGO | WWW.THEDUCKINNCHICAGO.COM

 TIME: 25 MINUTES   **YIELD:** 4 SERVINGS

 Our love of SPAM® Classic and everything Korean led us to create a loving tribute to the cultural mash-up that is quintessentially American with a dish that America loves—Eggs Benedict.

INGREDIENTS

- 8 eggs
- 8 slices SPAM® Classic
- 8 ounces kimchi
- 8 bao buns
- 2 tablespoons sesame seeds
- 3 tablespoons scallions, chopped

FOR BIMBIM HOLLANDAISE

- 6 egg yolks
- 12 ounces butter, clarified
- 4 tablespoons BimBim sauce
- 2 teaspoons lemon juice
- 1 teaspoon salt

DIRECTIONS

1. Steam the bao buns.
2. Brown the SPAM® slices in a griddle until crisp.
3. Poach the eggs in simmering water with a dash of white vinegar.
4. Place 2 buns on each plate, top with SPAM® Classic and poached eggs. Top with BimBim Hollandaise and sprinkle with sesame seeds and scallions.

BIMBIM HOLLANDAISE

1. Place egg yolks in a stainless steel bowl and add 1 tablespoon of hot water to eggs.
2. Whip until frothy over a double boiler.
3. Add hot clarified butter in a steady stream until incorporated.
4. Add lemon juice and BimBim sauce and adjust seasoning with salt. Keep warm.

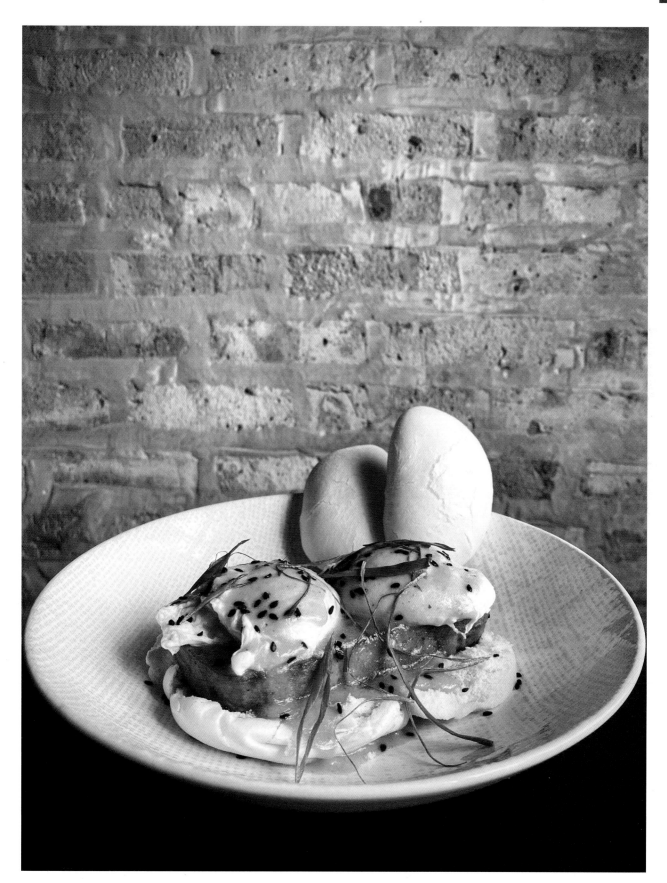

Grilled SPAM® Shady

SUBMITTED BY KIM WILCOX, OWNER AND CHEF, IT'S ALL SO YUMMY CAFÉ, KNOXVILLE, TENNESSEE
FACEBOOK: ITS ALL SO YUMMY CAFÉ/HILTON HEAD ICE CREAM

 TIME: 35 MINUTES   **YIELD:** 1 SERVING

 This sandwich was born on my way home from a music festival where a famous rapper was performing. I was humming to the song about his mom's spaghetti, and it came to me—a spaghetti grilled cheese with SPAM® Garlic!

INGREDIENTS

- 2 slices of hearty white sourdough bread
- 6 slices of provolone cheese
- 1–1½ cups of spaghetti (your favorite recipe)
- ½ can of SPAM® Garlic, cubed and pan fried
- Crushed red pepper
- Parmesan cheese

DIRECTIONS

1. Heat your cooking vessel to 325°F.
2. Warm up the spaghetti, add the pan-fried SPAM® Garlic, and set aside.
3. With your pastry brush, evenly spread melted butter on one side of each bread slice. Place the buttered sides down on the griddle. On one side of the bread, put 3 slices of provolone cheese. Repeat this on the other slice of bread. Spread the spaghetti on one slice of bread. It doesn't have to be neat; let it fall over the sides of the bread. Sprinkle the spaghetti with crushed red pepper.
4. When the bread is golden brown and the cheese has melted, about 3 to 4 minutes, use a sturdy spatula to put one half on top of the other. You can then remove the sandwich from the pan.
5. Garnish with Parmesan cheese, cut in half, and enjoy!

Hong Kong-Style SPAM® Classic and Egg Macaroni Soup

SUBMITTED BY LUCAS SIN, CHEF, JUNZI KITCHEN, NEW YORK, NEW YORK
CHEF'S INSTAGRAM: @LUCAS.SIN | RESTAURANT'S INSTAGRAM: @JUNZIKITCHEN | WWW.JUNZI.KITCHEN

TIME: 20 MINUTES **YIELD:** 4-6 SERVINGS

This is a dish served at *every* Hong Kong *cha chaan teng*, or Hong Kong-style diner, invented by the good people of Hong Kong during British colonial years. Hong Kong-style Western cuisine grew in response to British colonization, motivated by local aspirations to eat luxuriously with a modest budget. This SPAM® Classic, egg, and macaroni soup became a staple.

INGREDIENTS

- 1 (10½-ounce) can cream of chicken soup
- 20 ounces water
- 2 tablespoons Shaoxing wine
- 2 slices ginger, ½-inch thick
- 2 cups elbow macaroni
- ½ can SPAM® Classic, cut into ½-inch slices
- 4 eggs
- Sesame oil
- White pepper
- Oil
- Salt

DIRECTIONS

1. Cook pasta in a large pot of boiling, salted water, stirring occasionally, until soft, usually 2 minutes over the recommended "al dente" time. Drain and set aside.

2. In a large pot, add cream of chicken soup, water, Shaoxing wine, and ginger slices. Bring to a boil, stirring occasionally. Simmer for 5 minutes over low heat. Adjust seasoning as necessary with salt.

3. Heat a pan over high heat. Add oil. Sear SPAM® Classic until both sides are just crispy.

4. In the residual oil, fry eggs sunny-side up until the sides are crispy and the egg white is just set.

5. Combine macaroni and soup in a shallow dish. Finish a small dash of sesame oil and white pepper. Top with SPAM® Classic and egg.

Crystal Wrap SPAM® Classic

SUBMITTED BY MARTIN YAN, CHEF AND TV HOST OF *YAN CAN COOK*, OWNER OF M.Y. CHINA RESTAURANT, SAN FRANCISCO, CALIFORNIA
FACEBOOK: CHEFMARTINYAN

 TIME: 30–36 MINUTES   **YIELD:** 8–10 LETTUCE CUPS

 Delicate in appearance and filled with flavor, these Crystal Wraps will be the jewels on your plate.

INGREDIENTS

- 1 tablespoon vegetable oil
- 1 teaspoon minced ginger
- 1 clove garlic, minced
- ½ red bell pepper, seeded and diced
- ½ cup diced carrot
- 2–3 fresh shitake mushrooms, diced
- ½ pound SPAM® Classic, cut into ½-inch cubes
- 2 teaspoons chopped fresh cilantro
- 2 teaspoons chopped fresh basil
- 8–10 small lettuce cups (iceberg or butter lettuce)

SAUCE

- ¼ cup hoisin sauce
- 1 tablespoon oyster-flavored sauce
- 2 teaspoons soy sauce
- 1½ teaspoons chili garlic sauce
- 1 teaspoon sesame oil

DIRECTIONS

1. In a small bowl, combine sauce ingredients; set aside.

2. Place a stir-fry pan over medium-high heat until hot. Add oil, swirling to coat sides. Add ginger and garlic and cook until fragrant, about 15 seconds. Add bell pepper, carrot, and mushrooms; cook for 2 minutes. Add cubed SPAM® Classic and stir-fry for about 2 minutes.

3. To serve, spread a little sauce in a lettuce cup, spoon in some of the SPAM® mixture, sprinkle with a bit of chopped cilantro and basil, fold lettuce around filling, and eat out of hand.

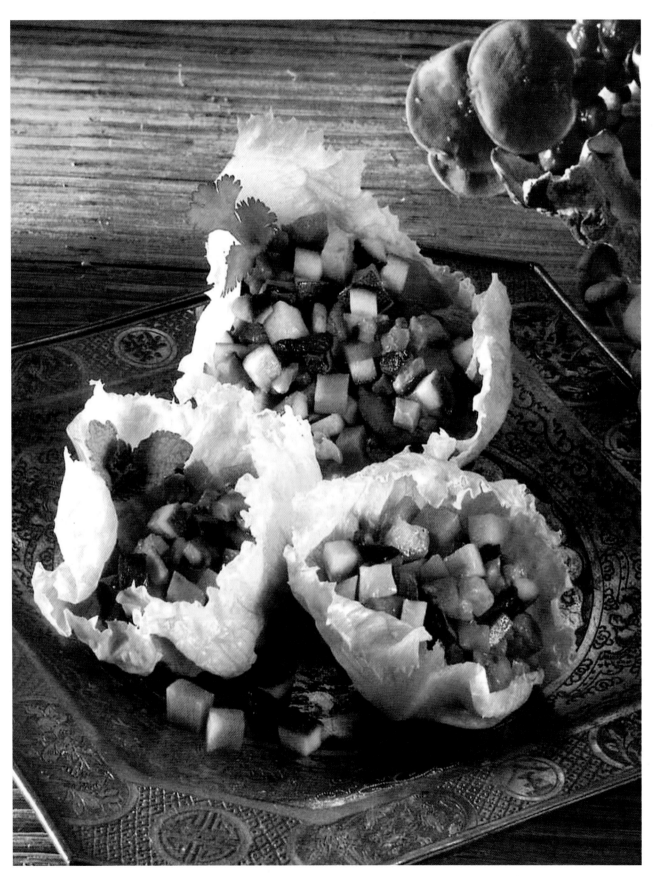

SPAM® Rice Pancake

SUBMITTED BY COOKAT
FACEBOOK: COOKATTV | INSTAGRAM: @COOKAT__ | YOUTUBE: COOKAT

 TIME: 20 MINUTES **YIELD:** 2 SERVINGS

 SPAM® Rice Pancake is one of Cookat's yummiest SPAM® Classic recipes! It is basically fried rice that is packed inside the SPAM® Classic slice. It's an easy recipe especially good for picnics or camping.

INGREDIENTS

- 2 cans SPAM® Classic
- 1 portion rice
- 3 eggs
- 3 tablespoons cubed SPAM® Classic
- 3 tablespoons chopped onion
- 2 teaspoons chopped jalapeño
- 2 teaspoons chopped spring onion
- 2 teaspoons canned corn
- Pinch of salt and pepper

DIRECTIONS

1. Cut 2 cans of SPAM® Classic into about ½-inch-thick slices. Cut out the center into a square shape.
2. Put the rice, jalapeño, onion, spring onion, corn, cubed SPAM® Classic, eggs, and salt in a bowl, and mix well.
3. Prepare a sauté pan and put square-shaped SPAM® slices on the pan. Then place the rice mixture inside each square, and cook until both sides turn light brown.
4. Enjoy it with some ramen, or by itself.

Wonton SPAM® Eggroll

SUBMITTED BY MICHAEL POLITZ, FOUNDER AND PUBLISHER, *FOOD & BEVERAGE MAGAZINE*
RECIPE BY JOSH GREEN, CORPORATE EXECUTIVE CHEF, *FOOD & BEVERAGE MAGAZINE* | FB101.COM

 TIME: 23 MINUTES   **YIELD:** 1 SERVING

 The egg roll has become one of the most popular Asian appetizers in America. We took the general concept and made it into a SPAM® Classic cheesy, flavorful twist on the traditional egg roll.

INGREDIENTS

- 2 wonton sheets
- 3 ounces pineapple, chopped
- 1 ounce chopped jalapeños
- 3 ounces SPAM® Classic, chopped
- 2 ounces Cheddar cheese
- 1 ounce cream cheese
- 1 egg

DIRECTIONS

1. Mix together the pineapple, jalapeño, Cheddar cheese, cream cheese, and SPAM® Classic in a bowl.

2. Lay the wonton sheets down.

3. Crack the egg in a bowl to make an egg wash.

4. Place the SPAM® mixture on the wonton paper. Spread the egg wash around the edge of the wonton sheet. Roll it up. Press the edges together.

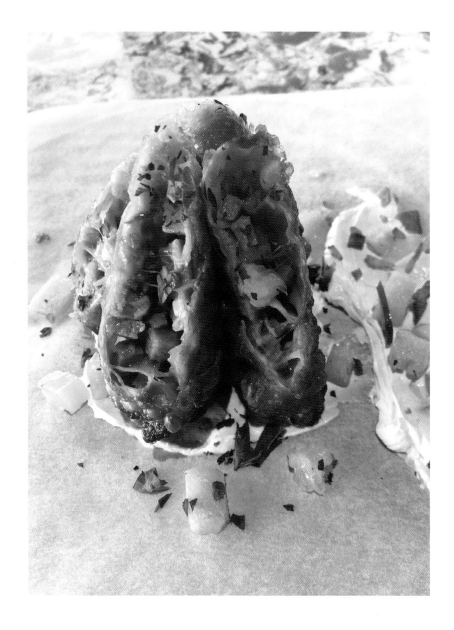

Wisconsin SPAM® Pierogi

SUBMITTED BY CYNDI HARLES, WRITER AND PHOTOGRAPHER AT BLUE RIBBON BLOG, WWW.STATEFAIRRECIPES.COM
RECIPE (ADAPTED) FROM KATELYN PELZEK, 2015 GREAT AMERICAN SPAM® CHAMPIONSHIP WINNER | WWW.STATEFAIRRECIPES.COM

 TIME: 1 HOUR, 30 MINUTES　　　 **YIELD:** 28 PIEROGI

 You'll enjoy these prize-winning SPAM® Classic pierogi dumplings filled with zippy sauerkraut and cubes of savory SPAM® Classic. The combination really works! The recipe comes from Katelyn Pelzek who won the blue ribbon in her division at the 2015 Wisconsin State Fair, Great American SPAM® Championship.

INGREDIENTS

DOUGH

- 3 eggs
- 1 (8-ounce) container sour cream (about 1 cup)
- 3 cups all-purpose flour
- 1 teaspoon salt
- 1 tablespoon baking powder
- 5 tablespoons butter, divided (reserved for searing stage)

FILLING

- 2 tablespoons butter
- ⅓ cup chopped onion
- 1½ cups sauerkraut (drained, squeezed, minced)
- 1 (12-ounce) can SPAM® Classic, diced
- Salt and pepper to taste

DIRECTIONS

1. To prepare the dough, beat together eggs and sour cream until smooth. Sift together flour, salt, and baking powder; stir into sour cream mixture until dough comes together. Knead on lightly floured surface until firm and smooth. Let rest ½ hour while making filling.

2. To prepare the filling, melt the 2 tablespoons butter in a skillet over medium heat. Stir in the onion, and cook until translucent, about 5 minutes. Add the diced SPAM® Classic. Sauté until browned, about 5 minutes. Add sauerkraut. Sauté additional 2 to 3 minutes. Season to taste with salt and pepper, then set aside to cool.

3. Divide dough in half, then roll out one-half to ⅛-inch thickness. Cut into 3-inch rounds. Place a small spoonful of filling in the center of each round. Moisten the edges with a little water, fold over, and press together with a fork to seal. Repeat this procedure with the second half of dough and remaining filling, re-rolling dough scraps as needed.

4. Bring a large pot of lightly salted water to a boil. Add pierogi. Cook 3 to 5 minutes or until the pierogi float to the top. Remove with a slotted spoon to a wax paper-lined surface.

5. Melt 1 tablespoon butter in the skillet over medium-high heat. Working in batches—about 5 to 6 pierogi at a time—sear until lightly browned, about 2 to 3 minutes on each side. Remove to a plate. Repeat with remaining butter and pierogi. Garnish with chopped, fresh herbs; serve with sour cream, if desired.

Fried Jalapeño SPAM® Poppers

SUBMITTED BY MICHAEL POLITZ, FOUNDER AND PUBLISHER, *FOOD & BEVERAGE MAGAZINE*
RECIPE BY JOSH GREEN, CORPORATE EXECUTIVE CHEF, *FOOD & BEVERAGE MAGAZINE* | FB101.COM

 TIME: 25 MINUTES   **YIELD:** 1 SERVING

 The jalapeño popper is so popular that it crossed the nation as a leading appetizer and party treat. My Aunt Shirley made the greatest stuffed jalapeños every holiday. We wanted to pay homage to this great lady and make a flavorful sweet, spicy, and cheesy SPAM® Classic interpretation.

INGREDIENTS

- 1 jalapeño
- 1 ounce SPAM® Classic, chopped
- ½ ounce Cheddar cheese, shredded
- Pineapple, chopped
- 2 ounces rice
- ½ ounce cream cheese
- 1 egg
- Bread crumbs

DIRECTIONS

1. Heat oil in a pot on medium heat until the oil reaches 325°F.
2. Fry the jalapeño for about 5 to 7 minutes. Remove it from the pot and cut off the top. Scoop out the insides but try to keep the rest of the jalapeño intact.
3. Mix together the pineapple, cream cheese, and Cheddar cheese. Stuff the jalapeño with the mixture.
4. Place the breadcrumbs in a bowl. Prepare an egg wash in another bowl. Dip the stuffed jalapeño in the breadcrumbs, and then in the egg wash, and then back in the breadcrumbs.
5. Place the breaded, stuffed jalapeño in the pot of oil and fry to golden brown. Place on a plate and top with cooked or uncooked (your preference) chopped SPAM® Classic and pineapple chunks.

Variation: SPAM®-Stuffed Jalapeño with Poached Egg

INGREDIENTS

- 1 jalapeño
- 2 ounces rice
- 3 ounces SPAM® Classic, chopped
- ½ ounce Cheddar cheese, shredded
- ½ ounce cream cheese
- 1 egg

 TIME: 1 HOUR   **YIELD:** 1 SERVING

DIRECTIONS

1. Cut a jalapeño in half.
2. Mix the rice, chopped SPAM® Classic (cooked or uncooked), and shredded Cheddar cheese and heat the mixture until hot. Stuff the jalapeño with the mixture.

3. Spread cream cheese on top of the mixture in the jalapeño. Place the stuffed jalapeño in the oven at 350°F for 5 minutes.

4. While the jalapeño is in the oven, boil a pot of water. Poach the egg, but make sure it is still runny. Remove the egg from the pot with a slotted spoon.

5. Remove the jalapeño from the oven and put on a plate. Top it with the poached egg.

Deviled SPAM® Grilled Cheese

SUBMITTED BY KIM WILCOX, OWNER AND CHEF, IT'S ALL SO YUMMY CAFÉ, KNOXVILLE, TENNESSEE
FACEBOOK: ITS ALL SO YUMMY CAFÉ/HILTON HEAD ICE CREAM

 TIME: 35 MINUTES   **YIELD:** 1 SERVING

 SPAM® with Cheese meets deviled eggs and creamy melted cheese, and it equals an ultimate comfort bite!

INGREDIENTS

- 2 slices of sourdough bread ½ inch thick
- 2 slices of American cheese
- 2 slices of Cheddar cheese
- 3-4 slices of seared SPAM® with Cheese
- 2 deviled egg halves (use your favorite recipe)
- Sweet-and-spicy spice blend

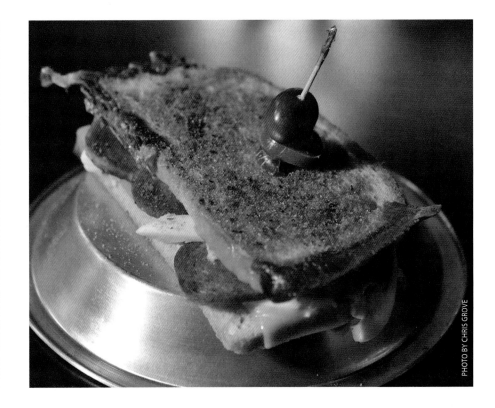

PHOTO BY CHRIS GROVE

DIRECTIONS

1. Heat your cooking vessel to 350°F.

2. With your pastry brush, evenly spread melted butter on one side of each bread slice. Place the buttered sides down on the griddle or in the pan. On one side of the bread, put a slice of American and a slice of Cheddar cheese. Repeat this on the other slice of bread. On one side of the bread, add 3 to 4 slices of seared SPAM® with Cheese, then add 2 deviled egg halves, chopped, on top.

3. When the bread is golden brown, and the cheese has melted about 3 to 4 minutes, use your spatula to flip one half of the sandwich onto the other half. You can then remove the sandwich from the pan.

4. Garnish with a shake of sweet-and-spicy seasoning, cut in half, and enjoy!

SPAM® Reuben Rollups

SUBMITTED BY CYNDI HARLES, WRITER AND PHOTOGRAPHER AT BLUE RIBBON BLOG, WWW.STATEFAIRRECIPES.COM
RECIPE (ADAPTED) FROM BEVERLY ZEHNTNER, 2014 GREAT AMERICAN SPAM® CHAMPIONSHIP WINNER
WWW.STATEFAIRRECIPES.COM

 TIME: 40 MINUTES   **YIELD:** 32 ROLLUPS

 With just 6 ingredients, this app-meets-meal is so simple to make. Plus, everyone who tastes them absolutely loves them. This creation has all the elements of a (nearly) traditional Reuben sandwich. You just swap out corned beef for your favorite canned meat!

DIRECTIONS

1. Mix SPAM® Classic, dressing, sauerkraut, and cheese together. Set aside.

2. Cut off crust of the bread slices. Roll out bread slices thin with a rolling pin.

3. Spoon SPAM® mixture onto bread slices (about 3 tablespoons each). Roll up and slice each into two parts. Coat with melted butter.

4. Bake at 375°F for 15 minutes. Serve warm.

INGREDIENTS

- 1 (12-ounce) can SPAM® Classic, chopped
- 1 cup Thousand Island dressing
- 2 cups canned sauerkraut
- 2 cups grated Swiss cheese
- 16 slices swirled rye bread
- ¼ cup melted butter

Fried Egg SPAMwich

SUBMITTED BY ELIZABETH'S KITCHEN DIARY, FOOD BLOGGER IN SCOTLAND
INSTAGRAM: @TANGORAINDROP | WWW.ELIZABETHSKITCHENDIARY.CO.UK

⏱ **TIME:** 30 MINUTES   🍽 **YIELD:** 8 SANDWICHES

 The chef and her son packed some simple provisions—a picnic blanket, a gas camping stove, a cast iron pan, an onion, a tin of SPAM® Classic, some sauce, some sun-dried tomatoes, and Parmesan bread rolls—and hit the sand and the sun. Frying the SPAM® Classic until it's nice and crispy gives it a fantastic texture. Its unique salty flavor goes really well with the fried onions and eggs. Yum!

INGREDIENTS

FOR THE SUN-DRIED TOMATO AND PARMESAN BREAD

- ¾ teaspoon instant dried yeast
- 3 cups white bread flour
- 1 teaspoon superfine sugar
- ½ teaspoon sea salt
- ½ cup Parmesan cheese, grated
- ⅓ cup sun-dried tomatoes, chopped
- 1 tablespoon olive oil
- 1 cup water

- 1 egg beaten, to glaze
- Coarse polenta for baking

FOR THE FRIED EGG SPAM®WICH

- 2 sun-dried tomato and Parmesan bread rolls
- 1 (7-ounce) can SPAM® Classic, cut into 6 or 8 slices
- 2 eggs
- 1 red onion, finely sliced
- Chili Ketchup, to serve
- Smokey Jalapeño Sauce, to serve

DIRECTIONS

1. Cover the sun-dried tomatoes in boiling water and leave to soak for 30 minutes before draining and chopping up fine.

2. Place all the ingredients, except for the beaten egg and polenta, in your bread machine in the manufacturer's recommended order and select the dough cycle.

3. Alternatively, combine the dry ingredients together, make a well, pour in the wet ingredients, and knead in the sun-dried tomatoes. Knead for 10 minutes, cover, and leave to rise until doubled in size.

4. When the dough cycle has finished, transfer the dough to a floured surface. Either divide into 8 bread rolls and place on a baking tray sprinkled with coarse polenta, or form into a single loaf. Leave to rise, covered, until doubled in size, about half an hour.

5. Using a sharp knife, score the top of each bread roll in an X, or slash across a single loaf, glaze with the beaten egg, and bake at 450°F for 15 to 20 minutes, until the bread sounds hollow when tapped. Transfer to a wire rack to cool completely, covered with a tea towel.

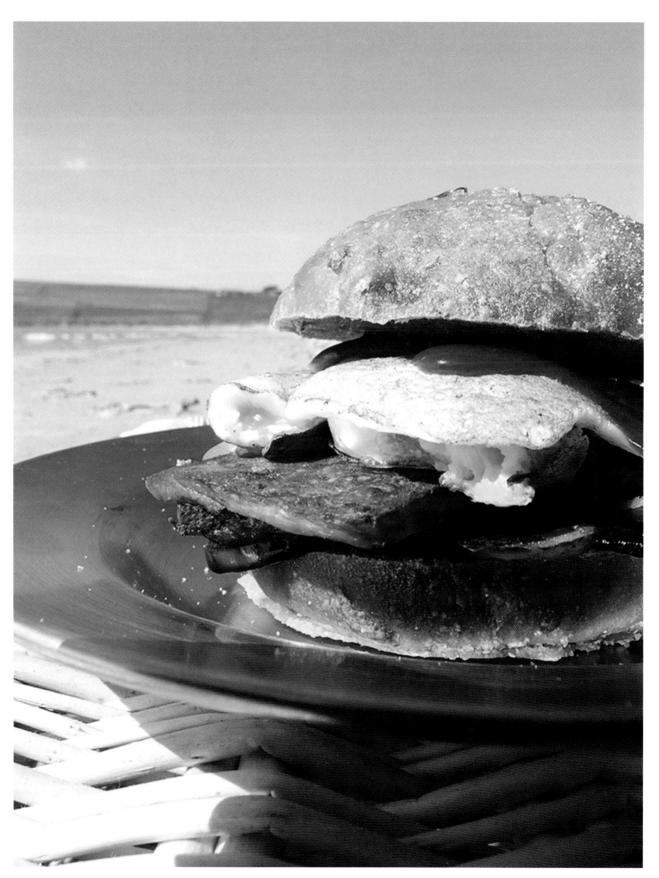

Sweet and Tangy Asian SPAM® Sandwich

SUBMITTED BY CYNDI HARLES, WRITER AND PHOTOGRAPHER AT BLUE RIBBON BLOG, WWW.STATEFAIRRECIPES.COM
RECIPE (ADAPTED) FROM JANE O'NEAL, 2013 GREAT AMERICAN SPAM® CHAMPIONSHIP WINNER | WWW.STATEFAIRRECIPES.COM

 TIME: 20 MINUTES   **YIELD:** 4 SERVINGS

 Enjoy the savory slices of SPAM® Classic nestled in a Kaiser roll with a zippy carrot slaw. You'll be wowed with how easy and delicious this recipe is.

INGREDIENTS

- 1 clove garlic, minced
- 2 teaspoons sugar
- 3 tablespoons vinegar
- 2 carrots, grated
- ½ cup cilantro leaves, chopped
- 2 scallions, thinly sliced
- 1 (12-ounce) can SPAM® Classic, cut into 8 slices
- ½ cup hoisin sauce
- 4 Kaiser rolls
- 4 tablespoons mayonnaise
- 1 sliced cucumber

DIRECTIONS

1. Stir together garlic, sugar, and vinegar in a small bowl.

2. In another bowl, toss together carrots, cilantro, and scallions. Combine with vinegar mixture; set aside.

3. Sauté SPAM® Classic over medium heat until slightly crisp. Add hoisin sauce to pan for the final minute of cooking.

4. Split the Kaiser rolls. Spread mayo on each top half. Assemble sandwiches with 2 SPAM® slices each, carrot/vinegar mixture, and cucumber slices.

Cheesy Tomato SPAM®wiches

SUBMITTED BY HALEY NELSON, OWNER/WRITER, CHEAP RECIPE BLOG, WWW.CHEAPRECIPEBLOG.COM
FACEBOOK: CHEAPRECIPEBLOG | INSTAGRAM: @CHEAPRECIPEBLOG

 TIME: 20 MINUTES　　 **YIELD:** 12 SANDWICHES

 Here's a recipe that combines SPAM® Classic, cheese, and tomato paste: junk food axis of evil or awesome sandwich spread? It's a tasty, fast, and budget-friendly sandwich spread recipe for everyone!

INGREDIENTS

- 1 (8-ounce) box pasteurized processed cheese product
- 1 can SPAM® Classic
- 1 (6-ounce) can tomato paste
- Sliced bread, or hamburger buns

DIRECTIONS

1. Mash together the cheese, SPAM® Classic, and tomato paste. When the ingredients are evenly mixed and a mouth-watering shade of pinkish red, it's ready to spread and bake.

2. Place a generous portion of the spread on halved buns or slices of bread.

3. Bake at 375°F for 10 minutes. Bonus: This spread will keep in the fridge for days and satisfy cravings for as long as the bread lasts!

SPAM® Breakfast Ramen

SUBMITTED BY RAYMUND MACAALAY, OWNER/BLOGGER AT ANG SARAP
FACEBOOK: ANGSARAPBLOG | INSTAGRAM: @ANGSARAPBLOG | WWW.ANGSARAP.NET

 TIME: 20 MINUTES   **YIELD:** 2 SERVINGS

 Are you constantly searching for the ultimate breakfast? This recipe may just be the one! Ramen might be odd for most to eat during breakfast, but noodle soups are a popular breakfast item in Asia. And it's not so different from the rice porridges and even fried rice breakfast dishes that are popular in many parts of the world.

INGREDIENTS

- 1 (6.5-ounce) package ramen noodles, cooked according to packet instructions
- 2 spring onions, thinly sliced (white part and green part separated)
- 4 shiitake mushrooms, finely chopped
- 2 teaspoons grated ginger
- 5 cloves garlic, minced
- 2 tablespoons sriracha hot sauce, adjust to your liking
- 4 cups dashi stock
- 2 cups vegetable stock
- 2 tablespoons sesame oil
- Oil

FOR THE TOPPINGS

- 1 can SPAM® Classic, sliced
- 1 dozen cooked gyoza (recipe on page 193)
- 2 eggs, cooked sunny-side up

DIRECTIONS

1. In a frying pan, add a small amount of oil then fry SPAM® slices until golden brown. Remove the slices from the pan, cut into small cubes, and set aside.

2. In a pot, add a small amount of oil then sauté garlic, ginger, and the white part of the spring onions.

3. Add the shiitake mushrooms and cook for a minute.

4. Pour the dashi stock, vegetable stock, and sriracha hot sauce. Bring it to a boil then simmer for 5 minutes. Turn heat off then add the sesame oil. Season with salt.

5. Place the noodles in a bowl, ladle the hot soup into the bowls, and top it with sunny-side up eggs, gyoza, SPAM® cubes, and spring onions. Serve immediately.

Gyoza

TIME: 37 MINUTES   **YIELD:** 30-40 PIECES

INGREDIENTS

- Approx. 30–40 gyoza wrappers (round)
- 2 cups chicken, finely chopped
- ½ cup shrimp, finely chopped
- 1 cup cabbage, finely chopped
- 1 tablespoon cornstarch
- 1 tablespoon sesame oil
- 1 tablespoon light soy sauce
- ½ thumb-size ginger, grated
- 2 cloves garlic, minced
- 1 stalk spring onion, chopped
- Cooking oil
- ½ cup boiling water

1. In a bowl, mix all ingredients together except for the wrappers and cooking oil.

2. Ready your wrappers and place 1 heaping teaspoon of the mixture on one-half of the wrappers. Brush ends with cold water then fold and seal ingredients in the middle.

3. In a large, heavy pan add oil and pan fry gyoza. Cook for 2 minutes or until bottom is browned. Add ½ cup of boiling water, cover pan with lid, then cook for 5 minutes. If you don't have large enough pans, do this in batches and do not overcrowd. Remove from pan then serve with soy sauce.

SIR CAN-A-LOT™ Sandwich

SUBMITTED BY MATTHEW BRENNAN AND CORVETTE ROMERO, CO-OWNERS, SHAMELESS BUNS, VANCOUVER, BRITISH COLUMBIA, CANADA
INSTAGRAM: @SHAMELESSBUNS | WWW.SHAMELESSBUNS.COM

A popular pick at our Shameless Buns food truck! This SPAM® Classic sandwich uses Pandesal as the vessel, which is a sweeter bun, similar to a brioche or a Hawaiian sweet bun. They are pillowy, soft, and slightly sweet and develop a beautiful golden crust when toasted. Pandesal are ubiquitous in the Philippines and are typically eaten as savory or sweet options. We've provided recipes below for each part of this sandwich. Enjoy!

Pandesal

 TIME: 2 HOURS, 30 MINUTES   **YIELD:** 30 PIECES

INGREDIENTS

- 1 packet active dry yeast
- 1¼ cup milk heated to 110°F
- 4½ cups all-purpose flour, divided
- 1 teaspoon salt
- ½ cup sugar
- ⅓ cup canola oil
- 2 large eggs, lightly beaten
  Bread crumbs for dusting the Pandesal dough

DIRECTIONS

1. In the bowl of a stand mixer, stir warm milk, 1 tablespoon sugar, and yeast. Then let the mixture stand until foamy.

2. In another bowl, combine 4 cups flour and salt. Add eggs, remaining sugar, and oil to foamy yeast and milk mixture.

3. Slowly add flour and salt mixture to stand mixer bowl, stirring with a wooden spatula.

4. Attach dough hook to the stand mixer and knead dough at medium speed for 10 minutes. Continue to knead and sprinkle flour in dough for about 20 minutes until dough has gathered in the middle of the mixer.

5. Turn off the mixer and form dough into a ball. Place it in another bowl and cover with a kitchen towel. Let stand for at least an hour until ball has doubled in size.

6. Gently deflate dough and divide into 30 pieces on 1 or 2 large baking sheets lined with parchment paper. Smooth and shape each portion into a ball, about 2½ to 3 inches in size.

7. Roll each ball in bread crumbs and place on cookie sheet, leaving space between each ball. Cover rolls with kitchen towel and let rise again for 30 more minutes.

8. Bake Pandesal for 20 to 25 minutes until slightly golden in a 350°F oven.

Fried Garlic Crumble

 TIME: 30 MINUTES   **YIELD:** ½ CUP

INGREDIENTS

- 12 large peeled garlic cloves, sliced very thin
- ½ cup olive oil
- Sea salt, to taste

DIRECTIONS

1. Heat oil at medium temperature in skillet. Add 1 or 2 slices garlic. If they slightly sizzle when entering the oil, you're ready to go! Add enough slices to cover the skillet in an even, thin layer, but do not overcrowd.

2. Lower heat to medium low. The garlic should be bubbling, but not gaining color too quickly. Continue frying and stirring constantly for 2 to 3 minutes until garlic has turned golden brown. Once golden brown, place each fried piece of garlic in a strainer over a bowl to drain. Season fried garlic with sea salt to taste.

3. Place fried garlic in a mortar bowl and grind with a pestle until ground. Do not over grind into powder! (You can also place in a bowl and use a long, round object like a rolling pin to grind.)

4. Place fried garlic crumble into an airtight container and store in a cool, dry location. The fried garlic will last for up to 2 weeks and can be used on sandwiches, salads, pizzas, pastas, and of course this Shameless Buns SPAM® sandwich!

Sriracha Mayo

 TIME: 8 MINUTES   **YIELD:** 1 CUP

INGREDIENTS

- 1 large egg at room temperature
- 1 tablespoon Dijon mustard
- 1 tablespoon white wine vinegar
- Kosher salt to taste
- 1 cup olive oil
- 1 teaspoon fresh lemon juice
- ¼ cup sriracha

DIRECTIONS

1. Crack the egg into the bowl of a food processor and process for 20 to 30 seconds.

2. Add mustard, vinegar, and salt. Process for another 20 to 30 seconds.

3. Scrape the sides and bottom of the bowl, turn the food processor on, and slowly add oil, starting with little drops. Once thickened and emulsified, add remaining oil in a slow, steady stream.

4. Once even thicker and looking like mayo, add sriracha, lemon juice, and additional salt to taste. Scrape the sides and combine all new ingredients. Process for an additional 20 to 30 seconds.

Atchara

Atchara is pickled papaya, plus julienned carrots, bell peppers, garlic, and ginger, among other things. A Filipino favorite!

 TIME: 45 MINUTES (pickling: 24 hours) **YIELD:** 12 SERVINGS

INGREDIENTS

- 3-4 pounds green (young) papaya, julienned
- 2 medium carrots, julienned
- 1 large onion, julienned
- 10 cloves garlic, minced
- 1 large red bell pepper, julienned
- 1 large green bell pepper, julienned
- 1 knob ginger, julienned
- 1 teaspoon salt
- 1⅓ cups sugar
- 2 cups white vinegar
- 1 teaspoon whole black peppercorns
- 4-8 bay leaves

DIRECTIONS

1. In a pot, boil the vinegar with garlic, bay leaf, sugar, black peppercorns, ginger, and salt for 5 minutes.
2. Place remaining ingredients in large container.
3. Once the ingredients in the pot are boiled, pour that mixture on top of the remaining ingredients. Mix everything together and cool for a few hours.
4. Place a sealed container with the atchara in the fridge and let pickle for a minimum of 24 hours. The atchara can be stored (refrigerated) for up to 6 months.

SIR CAN-A-LOT™ Assembly

 TIME: 8 MINUTES

INGREDIENTS

- 1 can SPAM® Classic
- Canola oil

1. Cut the SPAM® Classic into 6 thick slices.
2. Heat canola oil in frying pan. Once the oil is hot, place SPAM® slices in the pan.
3. Fry each side until both are golden brown and crispy (about 2 minutes per side).

SANDWICH ASSEMBLY

Build your sandwich in this order:

1. Shameless Buns TOP Secret Banana Ketchup (you can use your favorite bottle of banana ketchup, available at most Asian or Filipino supermarkets) on the bottom side of toasted Pandesal
2. Thick, fried slice of SPAM® Classic
3. Atchara (Pickled Papaya Slaw)
4. Sriracha Mayo Drizzle
5. Sunny-side-up egg
6. Thinly sliced green onion
7. Fried garlic crumble
8. Top of bun toasted and served adjacent to sandwich
9. Serve with SPAM® fries (see page 45)!

SPAM® Brand Inspiration
Why Chefs Love Using SPAM® Products

BETH ESPOSITO

A beautiful morning sunrise reminds me of the beaches of all the tropical islands I have visited over the years. SPAM® Classic and pineapple entice my food senses to complement a perfect breakfast overlooking the ocean!

Beth's Sprunch recipe is on page 156, and her SPAM® Horizons Bagel recipe is on page 158.

CHRISTIAN GILL

I grew up with red beans and rice, along with a can of SPAM® Classic. This dish is a match made in SPAM® brand heaven!

Christian's SPAM® Classic with Red Beans and Rice recipe is on page 159.

CHRISTY GOODE

I have always been a big fan of the SPAM® brand and wanted to create something that was fun and exciting but, most of all, tastes incredible.

Christy's SPAM® Scotch Egg recipe is on page 162.

CINDY KERSCHNER

I love the versatility of SPAM® products. It's fun using SPAM® Classic in my favorite recipes like stuffed peppers and breakfast burritos.

Cindy's SPAM® Pesto-Stuffed Peppers recipe is on page 164.

COOKAT

In South Korea, people love eating `SPAM® Classic and plain rice. We wanted to bring this delicious staple, with a unique twist, to an international audience!

COOKAT's SPAM® Rice Pancake recipe is on page 180.

CYNDI HARLES

It was a delight managing state fair recipe contests for the SPAM® brand for more than 15 years. Having first tasted SPAM® Classic as a kid when fishing with my dad, I never imagined back then my future role with the brand, and all the creative dishes people would win with over the years. These submissions are three of my all-time favorites.

Cyndi's adaption of Katelyn Pelzek's Wisconsin SPAM® Pierogi recipe is on page 182. Her adaptation of Beverly Zehntner's SPAM® Reuben Rollups is on page 187. Cyndi's adaptation of Jane O'Neal's Sweet and Tangy Asian SPAM® Sandwich is on page 190.

KATELYN PELZEK

This winning kid chef's mom says her daughter (Katelyn, 12 years old at the time) was inspired by enjoying SPAM® products and remembering family experiences at "Polish Fest" in the Milwaukee area, where German-Polish heritage is prominent.

BEVERLY ZEHNTNER

As a teen, Beverly often ate broiled SPAM® products with a glaze of brown sugar, mustard, and vinegar, as well as macaroni and cheese with SPAM® products. Now a mom with grown children that she also raised on SPAM® products, Beverly keeps the preferred pork around as a pantry staple.

JANE O'NEAL

Jane's winning dish came about from tinkering with a few of her family's favorite meals. Ultimately, she combined elements from a number of different dishes to create the winning Sweet and Tangy Asian SPAM® Sandwich.

DENISE DE CASTRO

I love eating quiche for brunch. It's savory and satisfying. And I love SPAM® Less Sodium! Full of flavor and easy to make, this recipe will impress your guests.

Denise's Mini SPAM® Quiche recipe is on page 165.

ELIZABETH'S KITCHEN DIARY

SPAM® Classic is a tasty, versatile, convenient, portable protein perfect for camping trips. It's great with scrambled eggs, fried in a bread roll, or even chopped up in a spicy camping chili recipe!

Elizabeth's Kitchen Diary's Fried Egg SPAM®wich recipe is on page 188.

GEORGEANN LEAMING

SPAM® products should be one of your pantry essentials! I was happy to show its versatility and how it can be used in so many recipes and cuisines.

Georgeann's Country Fried Chicken and Biscuits with SPAM® Classic Gravy recipe is on page 166, her Curried SPAM® Pot Stickers with Coconut Pineapple Sauce recipe is on page 168, and her Bulgogi SPAM® Bao Buns with Gochujang Slaw recipe is on page 172.

HALEY NELSON

I like cooking with SPAM® products because they are affordable, tasty, and can be prepared in so many different ways. Plus, the SPAM® brand has such an interesting history, dating back to WWII. Is there any food more American than SPAM® products? Also, my grandma used to cook with SPAM® Classic, and I love knowing that I'm enjoying the same foods as my grandparents did years ago.

Haley's Cheesy Tomato SPAM®wiches recipe is on page 191.

JONATHAN MELENDEZ

I grew up eating SPAM® products a lot as a kid and now, whenever I cook with it, it instantly brings me back to my childhood. Of course, now I'm eating it in much more sophisticated dishes like shakshuka!

Jonathan's SPAM® Shakshuka recipe is on page 170 and his SPAM® Corn Dogs recipe is on page 160.

KEVIN HICKEY

I love SPAM® Classic for breakfast, so I thought it would be great to create this Korean SPAM® Benedict.

Kevin's SPAM® Benedict with Kimchi and BimBim Hollandaise recipe is on page 174.

KIM WILCOX

I love taking fan favorites from our café and incorporating a SPAM® product as the star! These comfort food sandwiches are elevated to a new level with the addition of these favorites: SPAM® with Cheese and SPAM® Garlic.

Kim's Grilled SPAM® Shady recipe is on page 176, and her Deviled SPAM® Grilled Cheese recipe is on page 186.

LUCAS SIN

Just because certain dishes are simple doesn't mean they can't be thoughtful or careful or reference specific techniques and histories. This SPAM® Classic and Egg Macaroni Soup dish is a comforting staple from Hong Kong (China), where I'm from. And it's also one that tells the story of how American staples like SPAM® products have made their way around the world.

Lucas's Hong Kong-Style SPAM® Classic and Egg Macaroni Soup recipe is on page 177.

MARTIN YAN

The SPAM® brand has been a favorite in Hawaiian, South Korean, and many other Asian households. Delicious and versatile, it goes well with any ingredient in any kind of dish. SPAM® products have been a constant staple in my pantry for years.

Martin's Crystal Wrap SPAM® Classic recipe is on page 178.

MICHAEL POLITZ

I have always loved the concept of fusion cuisine. SPAM® products are a natural ingredient to add to any traditional recipe.

Michael's submission for Josh Green's Wonton SPAM® Eggroll recipe is on page 181 and Fried Jalapeño SPAM® Poppers recipe is on page 184.

RAYMUND MACAALAY

I cook SPAM® products because they are very convenient and very tasty. Just open the can and off you go!

Raymund's SPAM® Breakfast Ramen recipe is on page 192.

SHAMELESS BUNS

MATTHEW BRENNAN & CORVETTE ROMERO

SPAM® products played a huge part in the creation of Shameless Buns. We fell in love with the origin story of the SPAM® brand and its vital role in Filipino food history. The SPAM® brand is kitschy, colorful, versatile, and delicious—just like Shameless Buns!

Shameless Buns' SIR CAN-A-LOT™ Sandwich recipe is on page 194.

INDEX

Note: Page numbers in **bold** indicate contributor chef bios.

A

Adobo Fried Rice SPAM® Musubi Bites, 56
Adobo SPAM® Musubi, 57
appetizers, 42–73
    Adobo Fried Rice SPAM® Musubi Bites, 56
    Adobo SPAM® Musubi, 57
    Asian Inspired SPAM® Meatballs, 64
    Bacon-Wrapped SPAM® Bites, 65
    BBQ SPAM® Musubi, 61
    Bulgogi SPAM® Bao Buns with Gochujang Slaw, 172–73
    Creamy SPAM® with Real HORMEL® Bacon and Pasta Nachos, 48
    Curried SPAM® Pot Stickers with Coconut Pineapple Sauce, 168–69
    Deviled SPAM® Grilled Cheese, 186
    Fried Jalapeño SPAM® Poppers, 184–85
    Fried SPAM®ball with Spicy Ranch, 49
    Inside-Out SPAMTASTIC™ Musubi, 66
    Mini SPAM® Arepas, 52
    Mini SPAM® Nacho Burgers, 51
    Smoky Sweet SPAM® Maple Flavored Bites, 67
    SPAM® Classic Kimbap, 46
    SPAM® Classic Mini Korean Corndogs, 68
    SPAM® Corn Dogs, 160–61
    SPAM® Crunchy Nuggets, 53
    SPAM® Fries, 45
    SPAM® Guacamole Dip, 62
    SPAM® Island Appetizer, 55
    SPAM® Maple Flavored Baked Brie, 69
    SPAM® Musubi, 44
    SPAM® Musubi Crunchy Roll, 71
    SPAM® Pizza Rolls, 54
    SPAM® Reuben Rollups, 187
    SPAM® Summer Rolls, 59
    SPAMALICIOUS™ Fiesta Dip, 47
    SPAMALICIOUS™ Jalapeño Cheddar Biscuits, 50
    Spicy Chili Garlic SPAM® Musubi, 60
    Spicy SPAM® Bites, 70
    Teriyaki and Takuan SPAM® Musubi, 58
    Thai SPAM® Salad Cups, 63
    Wisconsin SPAM® Pierogi, 182–83
    Wonderful SPAM® Wontons, 72–73
    Wonton SPAM® Eggroll, 181
arepas, mini SPAM®, 52
Asian Inspired SPAM® Meatballs, 64
Asian SPAM® and Shishito Kabobs, 132
Asian SPAM® Slaw with Noodles, 106
Atchara, 197
avocado
    sandwiches/wraps/arepas with, 26, 29, 39, 52, 94
    SPAM® Guacamole Dip, 62

B

bacon
    Bacon-Wrapped SPAM® Bites, 65
    breads with (See bread)

Creamy SPAM® with Real HORMEL® Bacon and Pasta Nachos, 48
    Inside-Out SPAMTASTIC™ Musubi, 66
    SPAM® Breakfast Musubi, 20
    SPAM® Hawaiian Skillet, 125
    SPAM® Tater Tot Casserole, 127
bánh mi, SPAM® bánh mi, 92
Basic SPAM® with Ramen Noodles, 111
BBQ SPAM® Musubi, 61
beans
    SPAM® and Black Beans with Rice, 137
    SPAM® Classic Budae Jjigae Army Stew, 110
    SPAM® Classic Potato and Green Bean Sheet Pan Dinner, 141
    SPAM® Classic with Red Beans and Rice, 159
    SPAM® Maple Flavored Cowboy Beans, 142
beef, in SPAM® Classic and Beef Ramen, 77
"best by" date, 12
Bow Tie SPAM® Salad, 86
bread. See also sandwiches and wraps
    SPAMKINS™ Breakfast Muffins, 37
    SPAM® Baked French Toast, 28
    SPAM® Monkey Bread, 22
    SPAMALICIOUS™ Jalapeño Cheddar Biscuits, 50
breakfast, 14–41
    Country Fried Chicken and Biscuits with SPAM® Classic Gravy, 166–67
    Enchilada Breakfast SPAM® Casserole, 23
    Hearty SPAM® Breakfast Skillet, 17
    Huevos SPAM® Cheros, 25
    SPAMKINS™ Breakfast Muffins, 37
    SPAM® Bagel Sandwich, 27
    SPAM® Baked French Toast, 28
    SPAM® Benedict, 21
    SPAM® Breakfast Burrito, 26
    SPAM® Breakfast Hash, 19
    SPAM® Breakfast Musubi, 20
    SPAM® Breakfast Ramen, 192–93
    SPAM® Classic and Scrambled Eggs, 16
    SPAM® Classic and Spinach Mini Quiches, 31
    SPAM® Classic and Waffle Musubi with Spicy Maple Syrup, 41
    SPAM® Frittata, 40
    SPAM® Huevos Chilaquiles, 24
    SPAM® Loco Moco, 18
    SPAM® Maple Flavored Breakfast Bowl, 33
    SPAM® Maple Flavored Breakfast Poutine, 36
    SPAM® Maple Flavored Waffle Breakfast Sandwich, 32
    SPAM® Monkey Bread, 22
    SPAM® Sriracha Benedict, 39
    SPAM® Waffle with Cheese, 30
    SPAM® Western Omelet, 34
    Spiced Dutch Baby Pancake with SPAM® Figgy Pudding and Cranberry Butter, 38
    Top-of-the-Morning SPAM® Breakfast Bake, 35
    Ultimate SPAM® Breakfast SLT, 29

Brennan, Matthew. See Shameless Buns
broccoli, 84, 86, 111
brussels sprouts, 102, 143
Bulgogi SPAM® Bao Buns with Gochujang Slaw, 172–73
burritos and chiladas
    SPAM® Breakfast Burrito, 26
    SPAM® Chiladas, 138
    SPAM® Musubi Burrito, 128

C

cabbage, SPAM® Mahalo Cups, 89
Cantonese sweet and sour, SPAM®, 123
capers, fried, 67
Carrot & Cilantro Salad, 92
Cauliflower Rice SPAM® Musubi Tacos, 133
cheese
    Colorful SPAM® Skillet, 134
    eggs with (See eggs)
    Fried SPAM®ball with Spicy Ranch, 49
    pasta with (See pasta)
    sandwiches with (See sandwiches and wraps)
    SPAM® Huevos Chilaquiles, 24
    SPAM® Island Appetizer, 55
    SPAM® Maple Flavored Baked Brie, 69
    SPAM® Pineapple Cheesecake, 152–53
    SPAM® Pizza Rolls, 54
    SPAM® Waffle with Cheese, 30
    SPAMALICIOUS™ Fiesta Dip, 47
    SPAMALICIOUS™ Jalapeño Cheddar Biscuits, 50
    Spicy SPAM® Bites, 70
chefs' kitchens, recipes from, 154–97. See also specific chef's names
chicken, Country Fried Chicken and Biscuits with SPAM® Classic Gravy, 166–67
coconut
    Coconut Pineapple Sauce, 168–69
    Red Curry Coconut Sauce, 68
Colorful SPAM® Skillet, 134
Cookat, 180, **199**
corn and corn flour
    Mini SPAM® Arepas, 52
    SPAM® Corn Chowder, 99
    SPAM® Crunchy Nuggets, 53
corn dogs, 68, 160–61
Country Fried Chicken and Biscuits with SPAM® Classic Gravy, 166–67
cranberries
    Homemade Cranberry Sauce, 156
    Spiced Dutch Baby Pancake with SPAM® Figgy Pudding and Cranberry Butter, 38
Creamy SPAM® with Real HORMEL® Bacon and Pasta Nachos, 48
Crystal Wrap SPAM® Classic, 178–79
Curried SPAM® Pot Stickers with Coconut Pineapple Sauce, 168–69

D

De Castro, Denise, 165, **201**
desserts, 148–53
    Maple Brown Sugar SPAM® Ice Cream, 150–51
    SPAM® Pineapple Cheesecake, 152–53
Deviled SPAM® Grilled Cheese, 186
dinner, 108–47. *See also* chefs' kitchens, recipes
    from
    Asian SPAM® and Shishito Kabobs, 132
    Basic SPAM® with Ramen Noodles, 111
    Bulgogi SPAM® Bao Buns with Gochujang Slaw,
      172–73
    Cauliflower Rice SPAM® Musubi Tacos, 133
    Colorful SPAM® Skillet, 134
    Easy SPAM® Pho, 117
    General Tso SPAM® with Ramen, 135
    Juicy Lucy SPAMBURGER™ Hamburger, 124
    Polynesian Stir Fry, 136
    SPAM® and Black Beans with Rice, 137
    SPAM® Bo, 118–20
    SPAM® Cantonese Sweet and Sour, 123
    SPAM® Cheesy Macaroni Bake, 129
    SPAM® Chiladas, 138
    SPAM® Classic Bao Buns, 139
    SPAM® Classic Budae Jjigae Army Stew, 110
    SPAM® Classic Fajitas Sheet Pan Dinner, 140
    SPAM® Classic One-Skillet Mac and Cheese, 130
    SPAM® Classic Potato and Green Bean Sheet Pan
      Dinner, 141
    SPAM® Cordon Bleu Hawaii Kabobs, 113
    SPAM® Fried Rice, 131
    SPAM® Hawaiian Pizza, 115
    SPAM® Hawaiian Skillet, 125
    SPAM® Kimchi Fried Rice, 146
    SPAM® Maple Flavored Cowboy Beans, 142
    SPAM® Maple Flavored Roasted Brussels
      Sprouts, 143
    SPAM® Musubi Burrito, 128
    SPAM® Musubi Pizza, 144
    SPAM® Pizza Casserole, 145
    SPAM® Ramen Burger, 114
    SPAM® Tacos, 126
    SPAM® Tater Tot Casserole, 127
    SPAM® Teriyaki, Pineapple and Red Pepper
      Kabobs, 122
    SPAMBURGER™ Hamburger, 112
    Sun-Dried SPAM® Pasta, 116
    Surf and Turf SPAM® Musubi, 147
    Veggie SPAM® Skewers, 121
dips
    SPAM® Guacamole Dip, 62
    SPAMALICIOUS™ Fiesta Dip, 47
dumplings. *See* appetizers

E

Easy SPAM® Pho, 117
eggroll, wonton SPAM®, 181
eggs
    Enchilada Breakfast SPAM® Casserole, 23
    Fried Egg SPAM®wich, 188–89
    Fried Jalapeño SPAM® Poppers, 184–85
    Hearty SPAM® Breakfast Skillet, 17
    Hong Kong-Style SPAM® Classic and Egg
      Macaroni Soup, 177

Huevos SPAM® Cheros, 25
Inside-Out SPAMTASTIC™ Musubi, 66
Mini SPAM® Arepas, 52
Mini SPAM® Quiche, 165
SPAM® Bagel Sandwich, 27
SPAM® Baked French Toast, 28
SPAM® Benedict, 21
SPAM® Benedict with Kimchi and BimBim
  Hollandaise, 174–75
SPAM® Breakfast Musubi, 20
SPAM® Classic and Scrambled Eggs, 16
SPAM® Classic and Spinach Mini Quiches, 31
SPAM® Egg Salad Sandwich Spread, 100
SPAM® Frittata, 40
SPAM® Loco Moco, 18
SPAM® Maple Flavored Waffle Breakfast
  Sandwich, 32
SPAM® Scotch Egg, 162–63
SPAM® Shakshuka, 170–71
SPAM® Sriracha Benedict, 39
SPAM® Tamago Sandwich, 104
SPAM® Western Omelet, 34
Elizabeth's Kitchen Diary, 188–89, **201**
Enchilada Breakfast SPAM® Casserole, 23
Esposito, Beth, 156–57, 158, **198**

F

fajitas sheet pan dinner, SPAM® classic, 140
Fried Egg SPAM®wich, 188–89
Fried Jalapeño SPAM® Poppers, 184–85
Fried SPAM®ball with Spicy Ranch, 49
fries, SPAM® fries, 45
frittata, SPAM® frittata, 40

G

garlic crumble, fried, 196
General Tso SPAM® with Ramen, 135
Gill, Christian, 159, **198**
Goode, Christy, 162–63, **199**
Grilled SPAM® Shady, 176
guacamole dip, SPAM®, 62
Guam, SPAM® products and, 13
Gyoza, 193
gyros, SPAM®, 101

H

Harles, Cyndi, 182–83, 187, 190, **200**
hash, SPAM® breakfast, 19
Hawaii, SPAM® and, 13
Hawaiian pizza, SPAM®, 115
Hawaiian skillet, SPAM®, 125
Hawaiian SPAM® Sliders, 94
Hearty SPAM® Breakfast Skillet, 17
Hickey, Kevin, 174–75, **202**
history and evolution of SPAM®, 6–9
Hollandaise sauce, 174
Hong Kong-Style SPAM® Classic and Egg Macaroni
  Soup, 177
Hot Pressed Cuban SPAM®wich, 96
Huevos SPAM® Cheros, 25

I

ingredients, in SPAM® Classic, 10. *See also* main
  ingredients of recipes
Inside-Out SPAMTASTIC™ Musubi, 66

island appetizer, SPAM®, 55

J

Juicy Lucy SPAMBURGER™ Hamburger, 124

K

kabobs and skewers
    Asian SPAM® and Shishito Kabobs, 132
    SPAM® Cordon Bleu Hawaii Kabobs, 113
    SPAM® Teriyaki, Pineapple and Red Pepper
      Kabobs, 122
    Veggie SPAM® Skewers, 121
Kerschner, Cindy, 164, **199**
kimbap, SPAM® classic, 46

L

Leaming, Georgeann, 166–67, 168–69, 172–73, **201**
loco moco, SPAM® loco moco, 18
LONO Spring Roll Musubi, 97
lunch, 74–107. *See also* chefs' kitchens, recipes
    from
    Asian SPAM® Slaw with Noodles, 106
    Bow Tie SPAM® Salad, 86
    Hawaiian SPAM® Sliders, 94
    Hot Pressed Cuban SPAM®wich, 96
    LONO Spring Roll Musubi, 97
    Pineapple SPAM® Musubi Squares, 98
    Pulled SPAM® BBQ Sandwich, 80
    Savory SPAM® Classic with Ramen, 79
    SPAM® Bánh Mi, 92
    SPAM® Classic & Gnocchi Soup, 83
    SPAM® Classic and Beef Ramen, 77
    SPAM® Classic and Kimchi Fried Rice Balls, 107
    SPAM® Corn Chowder, 99
    SPAM® Egg Salad Sandwich Spread, 100
    SPAM® Fried Nice!, 76
    SPAM® Grilled Cheese with Brie and Peaches, 95
    SPAM® Gyros, 101
    SPAM® Kimchi Fried Rice Musubi, 85
    SPAM® Mac 'n' Cheese Musubi, 93
    SPAM® Mahalo Cups, 89
    SPAM® Maple Flavored Grain Bowl, 102
    SPAM® Panini, 103
    SPAM® PB&J, 91
    SPAM® Spuds, 84
    SPAM® Tamago Sandwich, 104
    SPAM® Western Pasta Salad, 82
    SPAM® Wild Rice Salad, 105
    SPAM®LT, 87
    SPAMBURGER™ Sloppy Joes, 90
    Teriyaki and Katsu SPAM® Musubi, 81
    Toasted SPAM® Classic and Cheese Sandwiches,
      88
    The 2-Step SPAM® Grilled Cheese, 78

M

Macaalay, Raymund, 192–93, **204**
mahalo cups, SPAM® mahalo cups, 89
Malt Vinegar Mousse, 67
Maple Brown Sugar SPAM® Ice Cream, 150–51
meatballs, Asian inspired SPAM®, 64
Melendez, Jonathan, 160–61, 170–71, **202**
Mini SPAM® Arepas, 52
Mini SPAM® Nacho Burgers, 51
Mini SPAM® Quiche, 165

monkey bread, SPAM® monkey bread, 22
mushrooms, dishes with, 18, 79, 110, 134, 145, 178–79, 192
musubi
  Adobo Fried Rice SPAM® Musubi Bites, 56
  Adobo SPAM® Musubi, 57
  BBQ SPAM® Musubi, 61
  Inside-Out SPAMTASTIC™ Musubi, 66
  LONO Spring Roll Musubi, 97
  Pineapple SPAM® Musubi Squares, 98
  SPAM® Breakfast Musubi, 20
  SPAM® Classic and Waffle Musubi with Spicy Maple Syrup, 41
  SPAM® Kimchi Fried Rice Musubi, 85
  SPAM® Mac 'n' Cheese Musubi, 93
  SPAM® Musubi, 44
  SPAM® Musubi Burrito, 128
  SPAM® Musubi Crunchy Roll, 71
  SPAM® Musubi Pizza, 144
  Spicy Chili Garlic SPAM® Musubi, 60
  Surf and Turf SPAM® Musubi, 147
  Teriyaki and Katsu SPAM® Musubi, 81
  Teriyaki and Takuan SPAM® Musubi, 58

N

nacho burgers, mini SPAM® nacho burgers, 51
nachos, 48
Nelson, Haley, 191, **202**
nuggets, SPAM® crunchy, 53

O

O'Neal, Jane, 190, **200**

P

pancake, SPAM® rice, 180
pancake, spiced Dutch baby, 38
panini, SPAM® panini, 103
pasta
  Asian SPAM® Slaw with Noodles, 106
  Basic SPAM® with Ramen Noodles, 111
  Creamy SPAM® with Real HORMEL® Bacon and Pasta Nachos, 48
  Easy SPAM® Pho, 117
  General Tso SPAM® with Ramen, 135
  Hong Kong-Style SPAM® Classic and Egg Macaroni Soup, 177
  LONO Spring Roll Musubi, 97
  Savory SPAM® Classic with Ramen, 79
  SPAM® Breakfast Ramen, 192–93
  SPAM® Cheesy Macaroni Bake, 129
  SPAM® Classic & Gnocchi Soup, 83
  SPAM® Classic and Beef Ramen, 77
  SPAM® Classic Budae Jjigae Army Stew, 110
  SPAM® Classic One-Skillet Mac and Cheese, 130
  SPAM® Mac 'n' Cheese Musubi, 93
  SPAM® Ramen Burger, 114
  SPAM® Western Pasta Salad, 82
  Sun-Dried SPAM® Pasta, 116
peaches, in SPAM® Grilled Cheese with Brie and Peaches, 95
peanuts
  Peanut Dipping Sauce, 59
  SPAM® PB&J, 91
  Thai Peanut Sauce, 66
Pelzek, Katelyn, 182–83, **200**
peppers and chilies

Asian SPAM® and Shishito Kabobs, 132
Atchara, 197
Fried Jalapeño SPAM® Poppers, 184–85
Polynesian Stir Fry, 136
Red Pepper Chutney, 162
SPAM® Breakfast Hash, 19
SPAM® Pesto-Stuffed Peppers, 164
SPAM® Teriyaki, Pineapple and Red Pepper Kabobs, 122
SPAM® Western Omelet, 34
SPAMALICIOUS™ Jalapeño Cheddar Biscuits, 50
pierogi, Wisconsin SPAM® pierogi, 182–83
pineapple
  Caramelized Pineapple, 162
  Coconut Pineapple Sauce, 168–69
  Pineapple SPAM® Musubi Squares, 98
  SPAM® Hawaiian Skillet, 125
  SPAM® Island Appetizer, 55
  SPAM® Pineapple Cheesecake, 152–53
  SPAM® Teriyaki, Pineapple and Red Pepper Kabobs, 122
pizza
  SPAM® Hawaiian Pizza, 115
  SPAM® Musubi Pizza, 144
  SPAM® Pizza Casserole, 145
  SPAM® Pizza Rolls, 54
Politz, Michael, 181, 184–85, **204**
Polynesian Stir Fry, 136
popularity of SPAM® products (locations), 13
pot stickers, curried SPAM®, 168–69
potatoes
  Hearty SPAM® Breakfast Skillet, 17
  SPAM® Breakfast Hash, 19
  SPAM® Classic & Gnocchi Soup, 83
  SPAM® Classic Potato and Green Bean Sheet Pan Dinner, 141
  SPAM® Pizza Casserole, 145
  SPAM® Spuds, 84
  SPAM® Tater Tot Casserole, 127
  Top-of-the-Morning SPAM® Breakfast Bake, 35
  Wonderful SPAM® Wontons, 72–73
poutine, SPAM® maple flavored, 36
Pulled SPAM® BBQ Sandwich, 80

Q

quinoa, in SPAM® Maple Flavored Grain Bowl, 102

R

ramen noodles. See pasta
Red Curry Coconut Sauce, 68
rice and wild rice. See also musubi
  Cauliflower Rice SPAM® Musubi Tacos, 133
  Fried SPAM®ball with Spicy Ranch, 49
  SPAM® and Black Beans with Rice, 137
  SPAM® Classic and Kimchi Fried Rice Balls, 107
  SPAM® Classic Kimbap, 46
  SPAM® Classic with Red Beans and Rice, 159
  SPAM® Fried Nice!, 76
  SPAM® Fried Rice, 131
  SPAM® Kimchi Fried Rice, 146
  SPAM® Loco Moco, 18
  SPAM® Pesto-Stuffed Peppers, 164
  SPAM® Rice Pancake, 180
  SPAM® Wild Rice Salad, 105

Spicy SPAM® Bites, 70
rolls
  LONO Spring Roll Musubi, 97
  SPAM® Musubi Crunchy Roll, 71
  SPAM® Pizza Rolls, 54
  SPAM® Summer Rolls, 59
Romero, Corvette. See Shameless Buns

S

salads
  Bow Tie SPAM® Salad, 86
  Carrot & Cilantro Salad, 92
  SPAM® Western Pasta Salad, 82
  SPAM® Wild Rice Salad, 105
  Thai SPAM® Salad Cups, 63
SPAMKINS™ Breakfast Muffins, 37
sandwiches and wraps
  Cauliflower Rice SPAM® Musubi Tacos, 133
  Cheesy Tomato SPAM®wiches, 191
  Crystal Wrap SPAM® Classic, 178–79
  Deviled SPAM® Grilled Cheese, 186
  Fried Egg SPAM®wich, 188–89
  Grilled SPAM® Shady, 176
  Hawaiian SPAM® Sliders, 94
  Hot Pressed Cuban SPAM®wich, 96
  Juicy Lucy SPAMBURGER™ Hamburger, 124
  Mini SPAM® Nacho Burgers, 51
  Pulled SPAM® BBQ Sandwich, 80
  SIR CAN-A-LOT™ Sandwich, 194–97
  SPAM® Bagel Sandwich, 27
  SPAM® Breakfast Burrito, 26
  SPAM® Chiladas, 138
  SPAM® Classic Bao Buns, 139
  SPAM® Egg Salad Sandwich Spread, 100
  SPAM® Grilled Cheese with Brie and Peaches, 95
  SPAM® Horizons Bagel, 158
  SPAM® Maple Flavored Waffle Breakfast Sandwich, 32
  SPAM® Musubi Burrito, 128
  SPAM® Panini, 103
  SPAM® PB&J, 91
  SPAM® Ramen Burger, 114
  SPAM® Reuben Rollups, 187
  SPAM® Tacos, 126
  SPAM® Tamago Sandwich, 104
  SPAM®LT, 87
  SPAMBURGER™ Hamburger, 112
  SPAMBURGER™ Sloppy Joes, 90
  Sprunch, 156–57
  Sweet and Tangy Asian SPAM® Sandwich, 190
  Toasted SPAM® Classic and Cheese Sandwiches, 88
  The 2-Step SPAM® Grilled Cheese, 78
  Ultimate SPAM® Breakfast SLT, 29
sauces
  Asian Honey Vinaigrette, 106
  BimBim Hollandaise, 174
  Coconut Pineapple Sauce, 168–69
  Homemade Cranberry Sauce, 156
  Maple-Orange Vinaigrette, 102
  Peanut Dipping Sauce, 59
  Red Curry Coconut Sauce, 68
  Red Pepper Chutney, 162
  Sriracha Mayonnaise, 68, 196
  Thai Peanut Sauce, 66

Vinaigrette Dressing, 105
sausage
    SPAM® Bo, 118–20
Savory SPAM® Classic with Ramen, 79
seafood
    Gyoza, 193
    SPAM® Bo, 118–20
    Surf and Turf SPAM® Musubi, 147
shakshuka, SPAM® shakshuka, 170–71
Shameless Buns, 194–97, **204**
sheet pan dinners, 140, 141
Sin, Lucas, 177, **203**
SIR CAN-A-LOT™ Sandwich, 194–97
sloppy joes, SPAMBURGER™ sloppy joes, 90
Smoky Sweet SPAM® Maple Flavored Bites, 67
soup
    Easy SPAM® Pho, 117
    Hong Kong-Style SPAM® Classic and Egg
        Macaroni Soup, 177
    SPAM® Classic & Gnocchi Soup, 83
    SPAM® Corn Chowder, 99
Southeast Asia, SPAM® and, 13
SPAM® products
    about: taste of products made with, 3
    ads through the years, 8
    "best by" date, 12
    history and evolution of, 6–9
    ingredients, illustrated, 10
    manufacturing process, 11
    popularity, worldwide locations, 13
    storing, shelf life, 12
SPAM® and Black Beans with Rice, 137
SPAM® Baked French Toast, 28
SPAM® Bánh Mi, 92
SPAM® Benedict, 21
SPAM® Benedict with Kimchi and BimBim
    Hollandaise, 174–75
SPAM® Bo, 118–20
SPAM® Breakfast Burrito, 26
SPAM® Breakfast Hash, 19
SPAM® Breakfast Ramen, 192–93
SPAM® Cantonese Sweet and Sour, 123
SPAM® Cheesy Macaroni Bake, 129
SPAM® Chiladas, 138
SPAM® Classic & Gnocchi Soup, 83
SPAM® Classic and Beef Ramen, 77
SPAM® Classic and Kimchi Fried Rice Balls, 107
SPAM® Classic and Scrambled Eggs, 16
SPAM® Classic and Spinach Mini Quiches, 31
SPAM® Classic and Waffle Musubi with Spicy
    Maple Syrup, 41
SPAM® Classic Bao Buns, 139
SPAM® Classic Budae Jjigae Army Stew, 110
SPAM® Classic Fajitas Sheet Pan Dinner, 140
SPAM® Classic Kimbap, 46
SPAM® Classic Mini Korean Corndogs, 68
SPAM® Classic One-Skillet Mac and Cheese, 130
SPAM® Classic Potato and Green Bean Sheet Pan
    Dinner, 141
SPAM® Classic with Red Beans and Rice, 159
SPAM® Cordon Bleu Hawaii Kabobs, 113
SPAM® Corn Chowder, 99
SPAM® Corn Dogs, 160–61
SPAM® Crunchy Nuggets, 53

SPAM® Egg Salad Sandwich Spread, 100
SPAM® Fried Nice!, 76
SPAM® Fried Rice, 131
SPAM® Fries, 45
SPAM® Frittata, 40
SPAM® Grilled Cheese with Brie and Peaches, 95
SPAM® Guacamole Dip, 62
SPAM® Gyros, 101
SPAM® Hawaiian Skillet, 125
SPAM® Horizons Bagel, 158
SPAM® Huevos Chilaquiles, 24
SPAM® Island Appetizer, 55
SPAM® Kimchi Fried Rice, 146
SPAM® Kimchi Fried Rice Musubi, 85
SPAM® Loco Moco, 18
SPAM® Mac 'n' Cheese Musubi, 93
SPAM® Mahalo Cups, 89
SPAM® Maple Flavored Baked Brie, 69
SPAM® Maple Flavored Breakfast Bowl, 33
SPAM® Maple Flavored Breakfast Poutine, 36
SPAM® Maple Flavored Cowboy Beans, 142
SPAM® Maple Flavored Grain Bowl, 102
SPAM® Maple Flavored Roasted Brussels Sprouts,
    143
SPAM® Maple Flavored Waffle Breakfast Sandwich,
    32
SPAM® Monkey Bread, 22
SPAM® Musubi, 44
SPAM® Musubi Crunchy Roll, 71
SPAM® Musubi Pizza, 144
SPAM® PB&J, 91
SPAM® Pesto-Stuffed Peppers, 164
SPAM® Pineapple Cheesecake, 152–53
SPAM® Pizza Casserole, 145
SPAM® Pizza Rolls, 54
SPAM® Ramen Burger, 114
SPAM® Reuben Rollups, 187
SPAM® Rice Pancake, 180
SPAM® Scotch Egg, 162–63
SPAM® Shakshuka, 170–71
SPAM® Spuds, 84
SPAM® Sriracha Benedict, 39
SPAM® Summer Rolls, 59
SPAM® Tacos, 126
SPAM® Tamago Sandwich, 104
SPAM® Tater Tot Casserole, 127
SPAM® Teriyaki, Pineapple and Red Pepper Kabobs,
    122
SPAM® Western Omelet, 34
SPAM® Western Pasta Salad, 82
SPAM® Wild Rice Salad, 105
SPAM®LT, 87
SPAMALICIOUS™ Fiesta Dip, 47
SPAMALICIOUS™ Jalapeño Cheddar Biscuits, 50
SPAMBURGER™ Hamburger, 112
SPAMBURGER™ Sloppy Joes, 90
Spiced Dutch Baby Pancake with SPAM® Figgy
    Pudding and Cranberry Butter, 38
Spicy Chili Garlic SPAM® Musubi, 60
Spicy SPAM® Bites, 70
spinach
    SPAM® Classic and Spinach Mini Quiches, 31
    SPAM® Classic Kimbap, 46
    SPAM® Maple Flavored Breakfast Bowl, 33

SPAM® Pesto-Stuffed Peppers, 164
    Top-of-the-Morning SPAM® Breakfast Bake, 35
Sprunch, 156–57
sriracha Benedict, SPAM® sriracha Benedict, 39
Sriracha Mayonnaise, 68, 196
stew, SPAM® classic budae jjigae army, 110
storing SPAM® (shelf life), 12
summer rolls, SPAM®, 59
Sun-Dried SPAM® Pasta, 116
Surf and Turf SPAM® Musubi, 147
Sweet and Tangy Asian SPAM® Sandwich, 190
sweet potatoes
    Smoky Sweet SPAM® Maple Flavored Bites, 67
    SPAM® Maple Flavored Breakfast Bowl, 33

T
tacos
    Cauliflower Rice SPAM® Musubi Tacos, 133
    SPAM® Tacos, 126
tamago sandwich, SPAM®, 104
Teriyaki and Katsu SPAM® Musubi, 81
Teriyaki and Takuan SPAM® Musubi, 58
Thai Peanut Sauce, 66
Thai SPAM® Salad Cups, 63
Toasted SPAM® Classic and Cheese Sandwiches, 88
tomatoes, in Cheesy Tomato SPAM®wiches, 191
Top-of-the-Morning SPAM® Breakfast Bake, 35
turkey
    Creamy SPAM® with Real HORMEL® Bacon and
        Pasta Nachos, 48
    SPAM® Gyros, 101
    SPAM® Mahalo Cups, 89
    SPAM® Pizza Casserole, 145
    SPAM® Spuds, 84
    Sprunch, 156–57
The 2-Step SPAM® Grilled Cheese, 78

U
UK, SPAM® products and, 13
Ultimate SPAM® Breakfast SLT, 29

V
Veggie SPAM® Skewers, 121
Vinaigrette Dressing, 105

W
waffles
    SPAM® Classic and Waffle Musubi with Spicy
        Maple Syrup, 41
    SPAM® Maple Flavored Waffle Breakfast
        Sandwich, 32
    SPAM® Waffle with Cheese, 30
Wilcox, Kim, 176, 186, **203**
Wisconsin SPAM® Pierogi, 182–83
Wonderful SPAM® Wontons, 72–73
Wonton SPAM® Eggroll, 181

Y
Yan, Martin, 178–79, **203**

Z
Zehntner, Beverly, 187, **200**